NOWHERE WAS SOMEWHERE

Nowhere was Somewhere

HOW HISTORY MAKES UTOPIAS
AND HOW
UTOPIAS MAKE HISTORY

BY

Arthur E. Morgan

Chapel Hill, 1946

THE UNIVERSITY OF NORTH CAROLINA PRESS

Contents

INTRODUCTION

The Significance of Utopia

ONLY A UTOPIA! HOW OFTEN HAVE PIC-
tures of a possible government and society been
dismissed with those words! Yet if we could follow the
threads of influence of the world's great utopias as they
have entered into the fabric of government and public policy,
we should come to have a high regard for the influence of
these designs of a good society which have appeared so
persistently through the ages.*

Utopias are as essential to human society as plans are essential for building bridges. During perhaps a hundred thousand
years men built bridges without conscious plans, but they
were mostly little bridges. Larger undertakings often failed
through unrecognized weaknesses, or, if they did persist, it
was often with extremely wasteful use of labor and materials.

When an engineer builds a great bridge he is creating
something the exact like of which never before existed. Yet
the cost of construction is so great, and the loss by failure
would be so serious, that cut-and-try methods are out of the
question. The very first effort must be successful. There

* The word "utopia" is used in these pages not only in its specific
sense but also with broader application, to include plans of government
or schemes for social improvement which present the possibilities of a
good society.

3

enters the need for design, which must be based on principles established by both theory and experiment. The success of this process is indicated by the fact that our country contains thousands of great structures, each one in its totality different from every other; yet each representing success of the first effort, as well as a high degree of economy and efficiency. Only with deliberate, intelligent, over-all design can economy be combined with effectiveness, and the full possibilities of available resources be realized.

For the most part societies have been developed much as men built bridges before the days of formal planning. For long ages, however, men have occasionally realized the inadequacy of cut-and-try methods. Repeatedly persons of creative imagination have given suggestions and hints of orderly social design. These are our utopias. Futile though they may seem, they have been in fact among the most powerful formative forces in history.

When a man or a people of tremendous energy and vitality appears, with a feeling of manifest destiny, great *power* of action is not necessarily associated with a correspondingly great *pattern* of action. If no sound pattern of life and of society is available, the drive of energy may expend itself in a whirlwind of destructive force, perhaps across the face of a continent, as was the case with Genghis Khan and his horde; or it may have a pattern without special excellence, as was the case with Napoleon. Where a great outpouring of energy is given form and design by a reasonably adequate pattern, then a great social structure may develop, as was the case in America when its people formulated and followed the utopia known as the Constitution of the United States.

"Human nature" has not the rigidly fixed character that commonly has been assumed. Rather, it has an almost unhampered teachableness, ready to learn and to adopt any pattern, whether good, bad, or indifferent, that is most effectively presented to it. The limitation is not with human nature, but with the quality of prevailing social patterns. The work of the utopian is to discover or to create better patterns, and to present them so effectively that they will win the acceptance of men.

The social structure of an anthill is inexorably fixed in the inborn nature of ants. There is almost no freedom of choice. In the design of human society, however, there *is* freedom. Contrary to the opinion frequently advanced by some Marxians, there is no single type of society toward which, through economic determinism or otherwise, all society is compelled to move.

The history of human society has been a history of diversity. No one type of organization has been exclusively dominant throughout the world and through the ages, and no one form includes all the values and excludes all unfavorable elements. Men's inherent impulses and make-up do not compel them to uniformity of social organization. As a result of this indeterminateness there has been, both in practice and in theory, a vast amount of exploration for desirable forms of social organization.

Not all types of society are equally conducive to a good life, and a social organization adapted to a people with one cultural background may be unsuitable for men with a greatly different tradition. The best combination of elements for any society probably has never existed, just as no bridge built by traditional methods ever was so nearly perfect that it could not be improved. So the designing of utopias goes on and has gone on since before men began to record their aspirations in writing; and it must go on, or social evolution will cease. Sometimes the utopian is not himself remarkably efficient as a man of action, though in a surprising proportion of cases he has been a person of notable achievements.

The great utopian has been like an oak tree in the forest, which year after year has striven to realize that perfect design which it is in the spirit of an oak tree to express, but without full success. A falling tree has broken its branches; other trees have crowded it, robbed it of its sunlight, and left it lopsided. Yet it persists, producing acorns, in each of which its spirit of perfection is transmitted whole and unimpaired. Perhaps some of these will grow in more favorable circumstances and come closer to perfection. The utopian has had in himself a vision and a pattern of a good society. In the adverse circumstances of his time he could not bring that design to fulfillment. Yet he feels it has innate worth, and he reproduces it in embryo in the form of a utopia, as the oak tree produces acorns, and he scatters copies broadcast over the earth, hoping that at least one of them may find a favored place to grow.

Men rarely exhibit sheer originality. Generally they do not create anew, but adapt and use what they have. When by chance, or in the achievement of ambition, or in a desire to serve country or mankind, a man or a group of men comes into great power and undertakes to create a new pattern of government, seldom does that new design originate in the minds of those in power or in the minds of their advisers. Men at such times commonly find themselves at an impasse. Here they are, with power to provide a new constitution for the state. A new order is needed. But no good pattern is suddenly revealed to them. What can they do? The most practical course, and the one which men in such positions generally follow, is to seize upon and put to use the most promising suggestions that are at hand, adapting them to the existing conditions, as Napoleon undertook to do with the "perfect" utopian constitution of the Abbé Sieyès.

More than most constitutions, that of the United States was a product of conscious, deliberate design. Yet, in so far as it was more than a codification of existing English and colonial practice, it was greatly influenced by writers of utopias, as well as by political economists such as John Locke. Rousseau's utopian *Social Contract* was influential in the formation of American policy. Such a major element as the separation of the legislative, executive, and judicial functions of government, which for a century and a half has been imposingly defended by judges and statesmen as a foundation of our liberties, apparently was taken, along with other important elements, from the most popular utopia of the time, Harrington's *Oceana*. This utopian pattern of government appears to have contributed substantially, not only to the federal Constitution, but, at an earlier date, to the constitutions of several of the thirteen states.*

* Because of a single reference by Madison in the *Federalist* (Home Library Edition, pp. 313-15), it has been commonly assumed that the idea of separate legislative, executive, and judicial functions was taken from Montesquieu. The following considerations (mostly from *Harrington and his Oceana*, by H. F. Russell-Smith, Cambridge University Press, 1914) point rather to Harrington's *Oceana*.

In the essay in which Montesquieu is mentioned, Madison refers to the provisions which were included in the constitutions already adopted by several states, for separating executive, legislative, and judicial functions. These provisions throw additional light on the question. John Adams, a fervent admirer of Harrington's *Oceana*, prepared the draft for the constitution of Massachusetts, which was adopted with few changes and has been but little modified to the present. As an indication that the parallel between *Oceana* and the Massachusetts constitution was not accidental or unconscious, in the convention which adopted the constitution the motion was offered and seconded that the word "Massachusetts" be expunged and that the word "Oceana" be substituted.—*Harrington and his Oceana*, p. 194.

William Penn probably was familiar with *Oceana*, and John Adams helped in drafting the post-revolutionary constitution of Pennsylvania. Of Penn's first constitution, Benjamin Franklin wrote that it "savored very strongly of Harrington and his *Oceana*." Adams also helped in drafting the constitutions of Virginia and New York, which partially follow *Oceana*. While the various state constitutions were being drafted, Adams' paper on constitutional principles, in which he discussed Harrington's *Oceana* and to a considerable degree followed it, was one of the relatively few commentaries which had general circulation in the colonies. When the federal constitution was drafted, it followed the

The American Constitution, offspring of utopias as it was, became itself a utopia to be taken, often blindly and uncritically, as the fundamental law of many other nations. Few other national constitutions have been so many times imitated.

This habit of using utopias in building constitutions did not begin in America. It is at least as old as European history. In the days of Greater Greece, when colonies were being planted from Spain to the Black Sea, constitutions and codes were designed for them, sometimes apparently more philosophical and utopian than the American Constitution. Also, colonies begun in the great periods of India grew into empires and lasted for many centuries. Some of these, too, had "utopian" constitutions prepared for them in advance. The French Revolution, the socialist movement, and the Constitution of Soviet Russia are in considerable degree examples of the reflection of utopian thinking and writing on the course of events, and the process is as old as recorded history.

Among the utopias and utopian writings which have powerfully influenced fundamental state policies are Plato's *Republic*, Plutarch's idealized *Lycurgus*, St. Augustine's *City of God*, More's *Utopia*, Campanella's *City of the Sun*, Andreae's *Christianopolis*, Harrington's *Oceana*, Rousseau's *Social Contract*, Robert Owen's utopian writings summed up in *The Book of the New Moral World*, and Bellamy's *Looking*

---

majority of the states in important respects, such as separation of legislative, executive, and judicial functions.

Oceana was published in 1656, the first constitution of Pennsylvania in 1682, and Montesquieu's *Spirit of Laws* in 1748. According to Russell-Smith, "Montesquieu was certainly acquainted with Harrington. In one place he coupled him with Plato, Aristotle, Machiavelli, and More."

These facts tend to the conclusion that it was Harrington's *Oceana*, more than Montesquieu's *Spirit of Laws*, which was the primary source of those provisions in the state and federal constitutions that follow the pattern of Harrington's utopian writing.

Backward. These books do not by any means exhaust the list of influential utopias, but they are representative.

Not only in its Constitution but in its later development, the government and policy of the United States have been greatly influenced by utopian writing. Bellamy's *Looking Backward* largely crystallized and gave form to liberal thinking in America. It gave birth to the "Nationalist" movement, the principles of which in turn were fumblingly adopted by the Populist party. Then the Democratic party took over Populist doctrines and further infected America with them. William Jennings Bryan's famous "cross of gold" speech was but a paraphrase from *Looking Backward*.

The "New Deal" has presented to America new forms of social organization. Here, too, I believe we can be skeptical of the originality of the "brain trusters," and can with profit ask the question, "What utopias are finding expression?"

It may be that the long-range direction and import of the New Deal can be made much clearer by reading Bellamy's *Looking Backward*. This assumption is not simply wild conjecture. For instance, Adolf Berle, one of the earliest, most intimate, and longest lasting of the confidential advisory group, was very deeply influenced by that source. His father was a friend and disciple of Bellamy. He grew up in a family in which Bellamy was a prophet of light, and in which *Looking Backward* was somewhat like a family Bible. This man's personal expressions of economic policy correspond to the philosophy of *Looking Backward* to a degree which seems to preclude mere chance. Striking parallels may be drawn between *Looking Backward* and various important and detailed elements of New Deal public policy. It may be said with considerable force that to understand the long-range implications of the New Deal one must read *Looking Backward*.

When we have demonstrated that new patterns of government, where they are more than codification of existing practice, commonly are borrowed and adapted from utopias, we have only half an answer to the problem of the origins of constitutions. There remains the question, What are the origins of utopias? Are they "bolts from the blue," sudden flashes of creative imagination, new revelations from heaven, or are they the original products of sheer logic? If statesmen who suddenly find themselves in possession of power lack the creative quality to originate the patterns of government they need, are utopians a different breed of men? Do they have strange ability to draw wisdom direct from heaven, to pass it on to the practical heads of government?

The answer is no; utopians have no such power. Nature is extremely parsimonious of originality. Very seldom does she create something new on a large scale. Nearly always she works over and uses what she already has. Utopians are no exception to this rule. Very generally, as this book endeavors to show, the great utopias have borrowed from earlier utopias, until sometimes the trail is lost in the distant past. But the tracing of that course only postpones the answer to our question, even though, along the way, striking new elements have entered into the growing utopian pattern.

The great fact which we come upon in the course of our inquiry is that, in their beginnings, utopias are not solely the creations of men's fancies, or revelations, or the products of pure logic; but to a very considerable degree they are records of actual human experience. Though they may be dressed in modern garb and adapted to existing conditions, in their fundamental characteristics many significant utopias are largely pictures of societies that have existed. In some cases the facts are well known and undisputed. For instance, Harrington, before writing the *Oceana,* which so greatly influenced American constitutions, traveled over Europe observing the effectiveness of various forms of government, and came back to England with such great admiration for the governments of some of the Italian city-states that to a considerable degree they provided his pattern. Harrington, Montesquieu, and others also were influenced by accounts of the ancient, pre-empire Roman Republic. How few American statesmen, orating on the priceless values of the American form of government, are aware of their various sources!

Many utopian themes can be traced back into the distant past until they blend into the utopian visions of the Hebrew prophets or into legends of the Golden Age. Is there evidence that even here we have, not revelations from heaven, not just fanciful creations of the imagination, but faint records of actual human societies? The writer believes there is such evidence, and he has indicated its general nature in the chapter on "The Golden Age."

A no less striking conclusion refers to the origin of that great utopian tradition which began with More's *Utopia*. In many remarkable elements More's picture of society differs from all the utopias and utopian writings which had preceded it for more than two thousand years. To the European mind it presented something new under the sun. And for more than four hundred years after More wrote, men searched vainly for the source of those strange new elements. The writer takes the position that he has located that source. He finds it to be not in earlier utopian writings, so much as in the actual existence of a civilized society then almost totally unknown to Europeans. It is a telling comment on cynical critics of the foremost utopias of English-speaking peoples, More's *Utopia* and Bellamy's *Looking Backward,* that their appraisals of "impossible" and "contrary to human nature" have been applied to pictures of society which were generally true descriptions of actual societies operating with a high degree of effectiveness, over a vast area, and for a long period.

While imitation and adaptation have been the chief resources of utopians and social innovators, they have not been the only methods by which progress is achieved. For long periods men may improve their lot by accumulations of slight changes in the way of doing things. Then come combinations of great need and creative genius, to bring about fundamentally new ways of meeting those needs. The utopian in a measure has realized this. Instead of endeavoring to bring about a good society by an accumulation of small modifications in existing custom, he endeavors to appraise the long-range needs and possibilities of men and, free from emotional attachment to the past, undertakes to design a radically new way of social life which will meet those needs and fulfill those possibilities. Yet often this strikingly new way was not an original idea of the utopian, but was suggested by the example of some actual society.

Today as never before this process of fundamental analysis and radically new design is necessary. In the past century and a half, men have discovered or created the agencies which make possible the emergence of a great, complex social organism. These agencies include steam, electric power, mechanical transportation, complex machinery and mass-production manufacture, modern communication, corporate organization, and administrative technique. These are not the tools of individual men, but the organs of a living society.

Yet mankind has not settled upon any pattern of design by which these new and unprecedented organs of society shall be incorporated into a social organism. The time seems to be at hand when slight modifications of the social order will not suffice, but fundamental changes of design will be necessary. The world's recent titanic struggle was between varying ideologies, each of which aims at some sort of utopia, though it may be a perverted or distorted one.

Society today is more in a state of flux than at any time since empire and feudalism, several thousand years ago, began to supplant the small, largely isolated communities which had been the habitation of man perhaps from his earliest days on the earth. This present intensity of flux probably will not continue indefinitely. Society will crystallize into relatively stable forms, with new or old designs. Ability to use atomic energy enormously increases the necessity for adequate social design, though it does not equally contribute to our capacity to create that design.

How will those designs be determined? In some degree, by means of the newly developed scientific method, fundamentally new types of social structure may be created which are not reproductions of the past, as men invented and perfected the telephone and the radio instead of developing existing means of communication. Yet, though to an increasing degree scientific design may replace older processes of merely rearranging the patterns of life, the existence of actual cases often suggests to the scientist what he will search for. Would synthetic rubber ever have been invented if natural rubber had not pointed the way? Would synthetic quinine, synthetic indigo, or synthetic alcohol have been found if the natural products had not previously existed? Similarly, would the creative designs of utopians have emerged without the suggestions of historic cases? And would radically new governmental regimes begin without the suggestions of utopias?

In the field of actual government and social order, for long periods to come the social patterns men live by will be those which their dynamic but none too original-minded leaders find lying about ready for use. It has been the work of the utopians, borrowing from earlier utopians, from their actual experience, and from information about society, to select the most excellent elements from all recorded experience, to add whatever they can of creative originality, and to combine those elements into a design for society which will commend itself to the judgment of men.

The trouble with human society has been, not too much attention to utopias, but too little. Had the quest for a good society been more universal, more objective, more critical and discriminating, then the crude social systems presented to the world by popular heroes would seem naïve and unconvincing and would not gain the credulous loyalty of great masses. Where utopias have been held in highest and most discriminating regard, there society has been at its best. A knowledge of the history and characteristics of utopias is essential to anyone who would take part in the refashioning of political, social, and economic institutions. They constitute one of the greatest reservoirs of human experience and aspiration.

Thus we find a constant interaction between the ideas and dreams of men, and their actual achievements. Utopian dreams have vastly influenced practical plans for government, while the best that men have done in government and society has entered into the making of utopias. To trace the interesting course of this interaction is the aim of this volume. It introduces the reader to a process of social thought and action which, notwithstanding the many histories of utopias which have been written, is yet largely an unexplored field.

PART ONE

NOWHERE WAS SOMEWHERE

I

Model for Utopia

FOR OVER FOUR HUNDRED YEARS CRITICS of Thomas More's *Utopia*, and for over half a century critics of Edward Bellamy's *Looking Backward*, have held that these descriptions of a good society were only dreams, beautiful of course, but in reality quite impossible, being in conflict with human nature. Because of that assumption, "utopian" came to be a synonym of the visionary and impracticable.

What if the great *Utopia* of Thomas More was not a product of his imagination, but a generally representative account of an actual country and its social system? What if the social system he described had long been in actual and successful existence on a vast scale? And what if the self-satisfied conclusion of "practical" men during the centuries since More's day—that his *Utopia* is an impracticable dream and contrary to human nature—is controverted by the actual facts? What if, instead of a fanciful "nobody," the supposed narrator in *Utopia* was an actual traveler bringing back a true story of his travels? Would not such conclusions be startling? Yet they are strongly implied by a comparison of More's *Utopia* with the best historical records.

Thomas More's *Utopia* consists essentially of two separate works, with different themes. The first part, which is a criticism of English government and society, was written last. The second part is the story of a strange land of strange ways. The two parts are somewhat loosely tied together by placing a few paragraphs referring to Utopia at the beginning and at the end of the first part.

In writing his famous work More allowed himself to express more than one interest. He criticized the drift of English political and social policy. He discussed Plato's philosophy. Two friends, Linacre and Grocyn, recently returned from Italy with a knowledge of Greek, had begun to teach that new subject at Oxford, and More had been one of their earliest students. Later association with Colet and Erasmus stimulated his interest in the "new learning," and he gave expression to that interest in his book. He took liberties with time, place, and circumstance, making the description of the strange land carry whatever burden was on his mind. He did not hesitate to invent or improvise. Concerning the length of time More's informant spent in "Utopia," and concerning his varied activities there, much of fiction and invention is evident. Yet these elements are, on the whole, easily discernible and separable from the main theme.

The chief content of the second part of More's famous narrative is, in effect, a substantially accurate description of a remarkable economic and social order which was in existence when More wrote his book. If the similarities are more than incidental we can say that with the discovery of that strange society a new element entered the current of utopian thought.

Even more significant, and quite aside from the question of literary source, such a comparison is important as supplying explicit evidence that a utopia like that of Thomas More or of Bellamy is not impossible or "contrary to human nature." If substantially the social order described in More's *Utopia*— Greek for "nowhere"—actually was *somewhere,* in full, vigorous, and successful operation, the main question then tends to become, not whether such a utopia is possible, but whether it is desirable. And as we compare that remarkable economy with striking resemblances in the New Deal, we can have new light on both the possibilities and the price of such a regime.

At the time when Europe was slowly emerging from the so-called Dark Ages, there existed on the other side of the globe a great empire, several times as populous as England and more extensive than any state on the European continent, within whose borders there was more nearly universal economic security than the civilized world had known. This remarkable empire had been formed by the gradual consolidation, partly by mutual consent and partly by military power, of many separate communities which had strong and stable social and economic organization running back many centuries to primitive folkways. Most of the elements in this social economy had existed in these smaller units before they were united. As usual, military force did not create the social values, but consolidated and regimented them, and, in the end, perhaps contributed to their downfall.

Throughout this great super-community there was substantial equality and security, with neither poverty nor conspicuous wealth. The local communities were linked together in such a way that scarcity in any one section could be quickly taken care of from surpluses in other parts of the realm. After unknown centuries of the gradual development of small utopia-like communities, they united into several independent nations, of which the strongest began to annex the others until it became dominant. This empire rose rapidly between the year 1100 and the middle of the sixteenth century. Instead of submerging the underlying community culture as did feudal Europe, the dominant empire magnified and glorified it. Today we know this great empire by the name of ancient Peru, or the empire of the Incas.

Before entering upon the question of whether Thomas More acquired his utopian ideas from descriptions of ancient Peru, it will be helpful to have a brief view of this remarkable society. Fortunately, historians who during the past century have examined the copious Spanish records of that early civilization are agreed as to its principal characteristics.

Prescott,[1] Markham,[2] and Means [3] are the three principal students of ancient Peru who wrote in English. Their study and research span almost an entire century and tell a connected and documented story of that ancient empire. And so thoroughly did the first of them, Prescott, do his work that Means, the authority of our day, has said that except for a few points, which he discussed in detail, "Prescott's account of the Inca Empire and all that pertains to it is as good and as trustworthy as any modern account. . . ." [4]

Stretched along the western coast of South America, the Inca empire spread over an area so extensive that its farthest parts were almost as widely separated as Alaska and Florida. Its population probably was much greater than that of any European country of its time. Its government was more thoroughly organized than any then existing in Europe. Its great road system compared favorably with that of Rome at the crest of her power; its irrigation system made those of Babylon and Nineveh seem elementary; its postal system was far better than any in Europe. A comprehensive system of public storehouses, with a closely knit government administration, made it possible for the empire to function as an economic and political whole.

These ancient Americans evolved their complex economic, social, and political organization uninfluenced by the stream of European and Asiatic culture. They were so separated from the rest of the world that they lacked a written language, knew nothing of the wheel and the axle either for vehicles or machines, did not use the arch in building, and had neither horses nor cattle. In spite of these handicaps they developed varied and extensive public works. In the production and distribution of their consumer goods to give universal economic security, they succeeded more completely than any other nation of their day or since.

At the time of the Spanish conquest, the Inca emperor (called the Inca) and his subordinates had a power over persons and property no less absolute than that of the modern dictator of a corporate state, and the Inca's family gave conquering Spaniards the impression that they alone had created the system. But historical research has made it clear that the fundamental social and economic structure of Peru was not the invention of a shrewd ruler and his family at the top, but rather was the slowly evolved folkway of democratically organized tribal communities which had widespread existence long before they began to cohere into a great empire. According to Philip Ainsworth Means, "Enough is known today to banish forever the old idea, fostered chiefly by the Inca Garcilaso de la Vega, that all order, well-being, and social stability in the Andean area was due to the Incas. We know that the foundations of their polity were laid long before they rose to power." [5]

In discussing the origin of the public control of land, Means wrote:

The *ayllu* [tribe] from the earliest times was the cell of the social organism. .... But in every sort of state, whether small and simple or large and complex, the *ayllu* owned the land collectively, distributing the usufruct of it among the heads of the households in the *ayllu*. Under the Incas the *ayllu* continued to own its land collectively, but with this difference: all the land was not in the hands of the *ayllus*. Land was divided into three portions: one for the Sun, *i.e.*, the state religion; one for the Inca; and one for the *ayllus*.[6]

It is contended by some scholars that the later centralized absolutism which the Spaniards found was already bringing on its own destruction before the invaders gave it the final blow. However, conquests and changes of government through the centuries prior to Columbus had not changed the basic social structure, any more than military victories and political revolutions changed the general social pattern of Europe. Whether the particular dynasty of the day was about to fall, we cannot be sure, but in any case we have proof that social security under an economy of relative abundance existed in an earlier America, and we know something of how the dictators who gained control of that ancient system maintained themselves in power. In each respect the story has amazing similarities to certain present-day tendencies. The only nation in western South America which never succumbed to Spanish rule was that of the Araucanians of central Chile, who never gave up their democratic form of government.

In both agriculture and industry an all-powerful state exerted control. At the time of marriage—and by law everyone was required to marry at a certain age—each couple was given by the community a house and a plot of ground large enough to support them. Additional land was given as each child was born. As the family decreased in size its property was proportionately diminished. There was no mortgage problem, for a person could not buy new land or dispose of what had been assigned to him. In addition to paying a tax in the form of labor on the lands of the Inca, each person was required to contribute a portion of his time to work the lands of the sick, the aged, the widows and orphans, and the soldiers in active service. Idleness was a crime, but the habit of work was so deeply ingrained in the people that outward compulsion seldom was necessary. The people willingly accepted and fulfilled their responsibilities.

Not only was soil erosion combated by the Inca and his subjects, much as by our Department of Agriculture conservationists, but a large part of the cultivated tracts were actually created by prodigious labor. Since much of their country consisted of steep, rocky mountain slopes, they laboriously built stone terraces and filled the spaces behind them with broken stone, covered by a layer of soil on which they raised crops. Over thousands of square miles of rugged mountainsides these terraces were so well built that they have survived four centuries of disuse.

The Peruvians appreciated the importance of maintaining soil fertility and made extensive use of guano, the deposit of sea birds which was brought from islands off the coast. To safeguard the supply they carefully regulated the way in which it should be exploited, and protected the birds with a no-hunting game law, the violation of which brought death.

Technically the most difficult agricultural problem was that of securing water for the dry lands along the coast. Over a wide area of the country the Incas built a great network of aqueducts and irrigation canals to bring water from the streams high in the interior down along the arid western slopes and to the coastal desert. Where irrigation was impossible they dug depressions in the desert sands, until ground moisture was reached. Then they heavily fertilized the bottoms and turned them into productive gardens. Thus these people took a region of barren desert and steep mountainsides, transformed it into a land of fabulous wealth, and used that wealth to provide economic security for all the people.

The great flocks of llamas scattered over the high mountain pastures of the Andes were the property of the state. Each year the Inca's officers organized enormous hunting parties. They surrounded large areas, gradually driving all animals toward a center. There they killed the wild beasts which preyed on the flock, and then sheared the llamas. The wool was stored in public warehouses, from which it was distributed to each family according to its requirements, for home spinning and weaving, or was allotted to supply the common needs. Cotton, produced in the low country, also was state property and was likewise distributed according to need.

Underneath the ceremonial of presenting goods to the Sun God and to the Inca, the Peruvian system of public store-houses was essentially comparable to certain features of the New Deal. The sick, the aged, the widowed were supplied from these surpluses, as many American families on relief have been given potatoes, oranges, and other products by the Surplus Commodity Corporation. Moreover, like Henry A. Wallace's "ever-normal granary" plan, large surpluses of corn and other products of good crop years were held over in a vast system of warehouses, to be distributed at the time of poor harvests.

All mining and all manufacturing except the simple craft production for home use were state undertakings. As the people of different sections of the country had developed skills for particular occupations, it was customary to assign woodworking to one district, metal crafts to another, and so on. Road maintenance and mining were the responsibility of the people who lived near where the work was done. Within each district there was frequent rotation of tasks, so that no person should be burdened with an undue share of labor, or should have to neglect the care of his own household. Most goods for food, clothing, and shelter were produced locally, so that the burden of transportation, which was on men's backs or on the backs of llamas, was held to a minimum. There was no system of money wages, but all who worked for the state were supplied with what they needed from public warehouses.

To operate this moneyless economy so that no one should be in want, the Peruvians practiced comprehensive industrial and agricultural planning and exercised continuing government regulation. A vital statistics bureau kept a careful record of all births and deaths, dividing the population into ten classes according to age, and thus the actual number and character of the population was determined annually. Each age class between sixteen and sixty had its own responsibilities.

From time to time there was conducted a comprehensive inventory of the resources and needs of the nation, including the amount of goods of every description in the public store-houses, the quantity and quality of farm land available and the use to which it was put, the mineral deposits which were or could be exploited, the needs of the country for new roads and bridges and aqueducts. On the basis of information thus gathered, work programs were drawn up for the various districts—a sort of "regional planning"—and the local officials were given responsibility for assigning and directing individual work. At the end of each year the Inca sent his officers over the country to compile a register of the year's production in all the various branches of agriculture and industry. Thus he could check alike against tax evasion and local graft. Of greater social significance, this inventory enabled the government to determine where there was a surplus of any product and where a scarcity, and to arrange for periodic distribution so that there would be enough in all the sections of the land. So far as possible, local self-sufficiency was achieved.

A system of such complexity naturally demanded a considerable number of public officers and a high degree of administrative organization. The whole population was hierarchically organized into military-like formations with major departments of ten thousand, subdivided and re-subdivided into units of one thousand, five hundred, one hundred, fifty, and down finally to ten families. The officer at the bottom of the scale, who had supervision of ten families, preserved order among them, saw to it that they discharged their responsibilities to the state, and presented their grievances against the government to those in greater authority.

Judicial matters were handled in the various communities by local magistrates whose jurisdiction covered petty disputes and offenses. The district governor or some other person designated as a superior judge had the responsibility for trying persons accused of serious crimes. Since there was almost no private property, crimes against property were nearly nonexistent. There was no appeal from the decisions of either local magistrates or superior judges, but it was provided that all decisions should be recorded and forwarded to the capital. Thus the central government officials could keep an eye on the administration of justice throughout the realm, and could correct abuses as they arose. Furthermore, a board of investigators toured the country from time to time to gather first-hand information on the character of the magistrates and their work. In all things the central government seems to have had a sincere interest in the welfare of all the people. In the lack of a written language the vast numbers of census and inventory records were kept on "quipus," or knotted cords.

But by our standards there was a darker side to this picture. Secure though a man might be in subsistence, he had almost no chance to achieve more. When not working his own plot of ground, he labored always at the direction of the government. However, the lack of freedom of the average man in Peru probably was no greater than that of the feudal serf in Japan or Russia or eastern Europe of the same time, where far less concern was exercised for his welfare.

Over the life of the common man in Peru there hung always the shadow of war, but perhaps to no greater degree than before the amalgamation of many tribes into one empire. Like the modern totalitarian chieftains, the Inca took advantage of every opportunity to expand his dominions, and, like them, he made his conquests by political means whenever he could. Propaganda, persuasion, negotiation, bribery—all of these modern techniques of aggrandizement were well understood and regularly employed. If they failed to bring submission, then threats, and finally war itself, followed. And always the Inca was able to back up his threat. Throughout the land there was a system which amounted to universal military training. Drills were held periodically in each village, and in time of war as many men were conscripted as were needed.

One of the principal reasons for Peruvian military successes was the amazing system of communication. The Incas realized that they must have good roads for the swift movement of troops, and accordingly they built a network of highways joining the various regions. The two most important roads paralleled each other from the northern district to the southern part of the long narrow country, a distance of almost two thousand miles. One ran through the coastal lowlands, the other along the rugged mountain slopes. Each in itself was an impressive engineering achievement. The coastal highway was in large part an embankment raised above the sand, although in some stretches where drifting sand would obliterate any highway huge markers were erected to indicate the way. In the mountains the road builders many times made great cuts through solid rock. They built high fills across ravines and swung suspension bridges across rivers and canyons.

Along these roads every five miles or so was a post-house at which were stationed couriers, who ran their assigned five-mile stretches with great speed, passing on their messages to other couriers, and so on until a dispatch should reach its final destination. Thus a call to arms and other military information could be quickly transmitted by courier throughout the land.

The care of troops on the march was well provided for. At suitable intervals along the roads were permanent barracks, military warehouses, and food depots. With such thoroughness it is not surprising that for centuries the Peruvians were able to meet the formula for victory popularly credited to General Forrest—"to get there fustest with the mostest men."

Whenever expansion of the empire was resisted, the enemy

was plundered and starved into submission, but at every stage of hostilities the Inca held open the possibility of peace. William H. Prescott, in *History of the Conquest of Peru,* quotes one of them as saying, "We must spare our enemies or it will be our loss, since they and all that belongs to them must soon be ours." [7]

When the enemy had submitted, his property was carefully protected, and often the native rulers were left in control of their former subjects. Effective steps were taken to secure their economic and political amalgamation with the rest of the empire. First came the introduction of the conquerors' religion—sun worship. Then, with truly modern efficiency, a survey was made of the conquered territory's resources and a census taken of its population. From this information a program was prepared for dividing the land between individual and state holdings, and soon the entire pattern of Inca economics was applied. Armed garrisons enforced the new order, and meanwhile many young men of the old ruling caste were sent to the Inca capital to be educated to a loyal understanding of the system. Wholesale propaganda was directed at the masses to win popular support. By providing economic security and even-handed justice, the wise government made its conquered people feel that their incorporation into the Empire was not a misfortune.

If there were threats of disloyalty the government met them with calm assurance. Says Prescott:

When any portion of the recent conquests showed a pertinacious spirit of disaffection, it was not uncommon to cause a part of the population, amounting, it might be, to ten thousand inhabitants or more, to remove to a distant quarter of the kingdom, occupied by ancient vassals of undoubted loyalty to the crown. A like number of these last was transplanted to the territory left vacant by the emigrants. . . . In time, the influence of the well-affected prevailed, supported as they were by royal authority and by the silent working of the national institutions, to which the strange races became gradually accustomed.[8]

With any conquered group the "silent working of the national institutions" usually proved irresistible. Gradually they became docile and loyal subjects. They were allowed to keep their language for use among themselves and they could even have local affairs managed by their own leaders. They were assured a subsistence. But in the management of the economic life they were subjected to co-ordination with the economy of the empire.

By combining ruthlessness in conquest with justice and administrative skill in dealing with conquered peoples the Incas were able to weld together a vast territory. Out of diversity of skills and local resources they created higher standards of living and evidences of a great and expanding civilization.

The dictatorship of the Incas was far-reaching. No citizen could change his residence or even be married without royal permission. But this dictatorship was exercised with great mildness, good will, and concern for the general welfare, with the result that the people were contented and the government was popular. Means declares:

> ... however stern the Incaic rule may have been, it was never unjust; however much the greatness and splendor of the highly placed may have been served and enhanced, the well-being of the humble was never lost to sight; however much may have been demanded of the people in the way of personal labor and of tribute, society as a whole was well compensated by the measure of peace and security, of plenty and of leisure, that was assured to it by the Incaic rule.[9]

Prescott has also testified, as in the following statement, to the generally beneficent character of the social organization:

The law was constantly directed to enforce a steady industry and a sober management of his affairs. No mendicant was tolerated in Peru. When a man was reduced by poverty or misfortune (it could hardly be by fault), the arm of the law was stretched out to minister relief; not the stinted relief of private charity, nor that which is doled out, drop by drop, as it were, from the frozen reservoirs of "the parish," but in generous measure, bringing no humiliation to the object of it, and placing him on a level with the rest of his countrymen.

... their manifold provisions against poverty ... were so perfect that in their wide extent of territory—much of it smitten with the curse of barrenness—no man, however humble, suffered for the want of food and clothing. Famine, so common a scourge in every other American nation, so common at that period in every country of civilized Europe, was an evil unknown in the dominions of the Incas.

The most enlightened of the Spaniards who first visited Peru, struck with the general appearance of plenty and prosperity, and with the astonishing order with which everything throughout the country was regulated, are loud in their expressions of admiration. No better government, in their opinion, could have been devised for the people.[10]

Spaniards of the conquest era would not have objected to features of the Inca systems which to people of a later day would seem tyrannous. Absolutism still held the field throughout much of Europe and Asia. The Peruvians had not learned how to apply democratic techniques to the government of a national state, but in that respect they were not greatly different from the nations of allegedly more advanced civilization. And in the satisfaction of the material needs of all the people they were certainly far more successful. We can well believe that the thoughtful European contemporaries who knew of the Inca system would have considered it ideal for the people who lived under it.

Several conditions contributed to the sudden downfall of this far-flung empire. It was despotic, and thereby suffered decrease of initiative among the masses of the people. In some respects at least, the sacrifice of democracy which may have seemed necessary for the quick unification of such a vast empire was a source of fatal weakness. The only adjacent population of South America which successfully withstood the pressure of the Incas, and almost the only one which never was subdued by Europeans, was that to the south of Peru, a people which maintained its primitive democracy. The people of Peru had become so used to accepting dictation from above that when strange men, by a curious turn of fate, got control of the Inca, the sole recognized source of public initiative was in foreign hands.

Another developing source of weakness was that while the people practiced monogamy in accordance with ancient democratic usage, the sacred Incas, considered above mere human morality, had of late departed from the ways of their fathers and indulged in many wives. There followed the inevitable jealousy and rivalry of the sons of different mothers. At the time of the Spanish conquest two half-brothers were at open war with each other for possession of supreme power, and the loyalty of the empire was divided.

The nation grew so vast, and with such rapidity, that unity was strained. More important still, all organization was vertical, to and from the Inca. There was little if any connection between officials of equal rank. They did not consult with each other, but reported to superiors. This policy may have prevented sedition and rebellion, but it also prevented the people's working together, except through the Inca. When a little band of Spanish adventurers captured him by perfidy in the guise of friendship, they could through him give orders to the entire Empire. Since the Inca was sacred, none of his subjects dared question his orders, even when he was prisoner. Thus a hundred and fifty adventurers got control of an empire, though the Inca's army of fifty thousand was close at hand. Had the Inca himself not been captured by supposedly friendly guests, his armies might have withstood the entire Spanish power.

We cannot judge the merit of the ancient Peruvian economy by the fact that the Empire fell before foreigners. The Aztec government of Mexico had a money economy and commerce. It had social classes, with social and economic inequality. It was far more like Europe than Peru. Yet it too fell quickly before a band of Spanish adventurers.

Probably the fundamental cause of the fall of Peru—other than the factor of non-democratic control from the top—was that Peru theretofore had an isolated culture which had lacked occasion to develop effective adaptation to strange influences. This isolation resulted in lack of resistance to common European diseases. As the Spaniards penetrated the country, fatal epidemics of diseases such as measles and chicken pox, to which Europeans were largely resistant, swept ahead of them, bringing not only wholesale death but the feeling of helpless terror.

Europe, Asia, and North Africa had interacted for thousands of years in war and trade and migration, and had developed versatility, sophistication, toughness, and a partial immunity to a great variety of evils. Though ancient Peru, keeping its organization extremely simple and uniform, throve in isolation, it fell quickly before the impact of strange European ways. Its failure seemed more the result of isolation and of its lack of democratic organization than the result of its unique economic organization. Could Peru have had a period of peaceful transition and adjustment to world-wide conditions, its remarkable economy might have survived and might have made a great contribution to civilization. As it is, Peruvian economy seems to have had its greatest influence on the world through the utopias which it inspired.

II

On the Trail of Utopian Sources

M Y FIRST INTEREST IN THE SOCIAL OR-
ganization of the Inca civilization of ancient Peru
developed during the writing of a biography of Edward
Bellamy. Search for possible sources of inspiration for his
utopian *Looking Backward* disclosed occasional references by
Bellamy and his immediate associates to the empire of the
Incas. Careful comparisons led to the conclusion that of all
his sources, ancient Peru was perhaps foremost in importance.

From Bellamy's *Looking Backward* the comparison led to
More's *Utopia*. The even more striking similarities between
Utopia and Peru resulted in the study reported in this and
the following chapters.* In order to leave no uncertainty in

---

* Louis Baudin in his *L'Empire Socialiste des Inka* points out that
few utopians have drawn upon Peru. Among these few he mentions
Campanella and Morelly, the first of whom, Baudin believes, got his
title (*Civitas Solis*, 1630) and possibly certain parts of his system from
Peru. However, a careful examination of the text of the "City of the
Sun" discloses little or no familiarity with Peru on the part of Campanella, while Campanella states that his City of the Sun is on the island
of Taprobane (Ceylon). His utopia suggests more definite acquaintance
with Tacitus' *Germania* and Plutarch's *Lycurgus*. Morelly mentions his
debt to Peru and includes in his system cultivation in common, public
storehouses, and roads "with country dwellings at equal distances along
the edge." In his book reviewing, Bellamy indicated familiarity with
Morelly.

the matter, it has seemed desirable to add case upon case of parallels between More's *Utopia* and the actual social order of this strange country—which had existed through the centuries unknown to Europe—until doubt as to Thomas More's sources would be no longer tenable.

It is known that shortly after 1514 More went to Flanders on a mission for Henry VIII, and that while there he visited Peter Giles, then secretary to the Municipality of Antwerp. More begins his *Utopia* by stating that while he was in Antwerp Giles introduced him to one Raphael Hythloday, who, he wrote, had sailed on three of the reputed four voyages of Amerigo Vespucci. On the "fourth" of these reputed voyages (to the east coast of South America in 1503), according to More's story, Hythloday left the ship "at the farthest place at which they touched," and with five comrades and an escort of natives traveled overland to Utopia. The episode of the men's being left behind corresponds to the account presumably written by Vespucci.

For four hundred years this introduction to *Utopia* has been thought of as purely fanciful. However, if we treat it as simply a factual account we find a story of great interest. In this chapter we will touch but briefly on the evidence that More could have received direct information from Peru. Yet, because it has been generally supposed that he could not have known of the Incas, the evidence is presented at greater length in an appendix. This of itself is an interesting story of pre-Columbian and early post-Columbian voyages to America, and of three expeditions to Peru from the Atlantic coast, before Pizarro.*

There are several phases of the evidence which support the theory that More's book in the main is not a fictitious story, but a record of a trip to Peru and of what was observed there. In case the particular trip of Vespucci referred to by More had not been made, there were numerous other

* See Appendix, p. 187.

possible sources of information which might have been available for writing *Utopia*. There is strong evidence that several Portuguese voyages, both before and after Columbus, reached the east coast of South America in time to have met the conditions required by More's narrative.

We know now that Peru was first visited, not by Pizzaro on his trip down the west coast of South America, but from the Atlantic coast of what is now central or southern Brazil, and the route taken by the first historically recorded expedition is nearly the same, so far as brief descriptions indicate, as that taken by Thomas More's character Raphael Hythloday on his visit to Utopia.

More's description of the life and social system of Utopia corresponds in the main so closely with ancient Peru, both in major features and in small incidental details, that accidental coincidence seems to be out of the question. The statement in *Utopia* that Hythloday was not a common sailor, but an educated traveler, would help to account for the close observation and accurate, detailed descriptions of Peruvian life and economy which are found in More's *Utopia*.

More's brief narrative of the trip across country to Utopia fairly accurately conforms to what so short an account might be of the part of southern Brazil over which his traveler would have passed. The account in *Utopia* tells us that "after many days' journey they came to towns and cities, and to commonwealths, that were both happily governed and well peopled. Under the equator, and as far on both sides as the sun moves, there lay vast deserts that were parched with the perpetual heat of the sun," etc. If "Hythloday" had come along a Guarani Indian trade route to the region of Lake Titicaca, that is about the kind of country he would have found. The description would be accurate for ancient Peru so far as lands under and to the south of the equator are concerned.

On reaching Utopia, "The first vessels they saw were flat-bottomed, their sails were made of reeds and wicker woven close together, only some were made of leather." This is a very good description of the curious and unusual craft used then—and now—on Lake Titicaca. More continues, "but afterward they found ships with round keels and canvas sails, in all respects like our ships." The Peruvian balsa rafts on the Pacific did have cabins and canvas sails. They had keels, but not after the style of European vessels. (These balsa rafts are described more fully in Chapter IV.)

This narrative seems the more probably a factual account in the light of what we now know of the first acquaintance of Europeans with the Inca Empire. Any explorer reaching the east coast of South America and communicating with the natives almost certainly would have heard of that fabulous kingdom. Before Columbus' first voyage there were well traveled trade routes from the Atlantic coast to the land of the Incas. Gold and silver work from Peru had reached the Atlantic coast. Eastern Indians had gone to the land of the Incas, while in one case at least it seems that one of the Inca people visited a fleet which returned to Europe two years before More wrote *Utopia*. Chickens, imported to the eastern coast of South America by Europeans, had been passed across the continent by traders to Peru before the Inca Empire was discovered from the Pacific. A suggestion that Vespucci heard of the Incas on his long voyage in 1502 is supplied in the account of his trip which is accepted as authentic: "The people of the country talk about gold and other metals and drugs and many miracles, but I am from St. Thomas, and time will tell all."

Philip Ainsworth Means, in his book *The Spanish Main*, tells how in 1515 and 1516 Dias de Solis, cruising along the coast of Brazil, probably picked up rumors of the golden kingdom. After the death of de Solis a few survivors of his voyage, on an island off the Brazilian coast, heard stories of the great potentate far away, called the "Great White King."

"With amazing courage," Means writes, "this little band of white men, accompanied part of the way by a large number of Indian auxiliaries, made their way westward across immensely difficult country, amid every sort of natural and human peril, until at last they entered what is now south central Bolivia, well within the dominions of the Inca." On the return trip all but two of them were massacred.

In 1525 Sebastian Cabot with two hundred men, supported by merchants of Spain, Italy, and England, stopped on the east coast of Brazil. The ostensible purpose of the expedition was to pass through the Straits of Magellan, but actually, it appears, they wished to search for the fabulous kingdom. Means quotes a Spanish authority as of the opinion that Cabot's expedition, at least, was stimulated by rumors of the Inca country which had reached Europe both from Panama and from the coast of Brazil. A party of fifteen went across country from the coast of Brazil to the land of the Incas, and were entertained by Inca officials. Only seven of the party returned alive. The route from the coast of Brazil to Peru taken by both these historic expeditions is approximately the same, within the limits of meager accounts, as that described by Thomas More in *Utopia*. The expedition of Dias de Solis in 1515 and 1516 was undertaken just at the time Thomas More was writing his famous book.

It is interesting that both More's account of "Raphael Hythloday's" trip across country to Utopia, and the old Spanish accounts of the trip of Dias de Solis, mention the expedition's being accompanied part of the way by a large number of Indian auxiliaries. In the case of de Solis, at least, that is recorded history. It creates a strong presumption that the Indians knew where they were going, along a familiar route.

In 1526 four Portuguese, with two thousand Guarani Indians from the coast, left San Vicente (now Santos) in southern Brazil, went to Peru on a raiding party, and returned to their party in Paraguay with much booty. The commander, Garcia, sent two of his men to Brazil to report. After they left, he and his party, except Garcia's son, were killed by the Indians.[1] During the past century there was discovered in the archives of the Fugger family a record of a voyage to the eastern coast of South America, with the return to Europe in 1514, bringing quite specific information about the wealth of Peru.

In support of the theory that several voyages were made from Portugal to the east coast of South America, on one of which More's informant might have been present, there is considerable historical evidence, which is discussed in the Appendix.

Not only is the organization of society presented by More in *Utopia* substantially identical with that of ancient Peru, but in curious, incidental ways which have nothing to do with the essential character of an ideal society the description of Utopia corresponds to the facts about the ancient empire of the Incas.

As already suggested, our chief present-day interest in the likeness of the country of Utopia to ancient Peru is in the fact that the elements of a social and economic order which ever since Thomas More's day have been dismissed as "utopian," meaning impracticable of attainment, did in fact exist and prosper for centuries, and for part of that time over a great domain. Other valid criticisms of Bellamy's and More's utopias there may be, but inherent impossibility would seem, judging by Peru, not to be one of them. Let us now turn to an examination of the social organization in Peru, in *Utopia*, and in *Looking Backward*.

In Peru, in *Utopia*, and in *Looking Backward*, the basic economic organization is the same. It is what Thomas More speaks of in *Utopia* as "*the foundation of all the rest, their living in common, without the use of money.*" The Peruvian system, like the system described by More, was greatly different from that of Europe or Asia. As already stated, there was no money, and almost no private trading except local exchange of surplus local goods such as were produced for home consumption. All production, except for family or local needs, was in the hands of the central government. All goods, except food and clothing produced by each family for its own use or perhaps for purely local exchange, were gathered into warehouses and then distributed as needed, "without money and without price." Except for the small hereditary ruling class, and perhaps for local officials, there was equality in distribution. This fundamental economic structure, which existed nowhere in Europe, is used as to its principal and controlling feature both in *Utopia* and in *Looking Backward*. Quotations from those two books and from Prescott's *Conquest of Peru* will illustrate.

OWNERSHIP OF LAND

Private ownership of land is eliminated. In Peru, after provision was made for the government and the priests, according to Prescott:

The remainder of the lands was divided, *per capita*, in equal shares among the people.

... not only did the lease, if we may so call it, terminate with the year, but during that period the tenant had no power to alienate or to add to his possessions.

A more thorough and effectual agrarian law than this cannot be imagined.

All the mines in the kingdom belonged to the Inca.[2]

When a man married:

... the community or district in which he lived furnished him with a dwelling. ... A lot of land was then assigned to him sufficient for his own maintenance and that of his wife.[3]

Note the similarity of the account in *Utopia:*

> ... the people consider themselves rather as tenants than land-
> lords. They have built over all the country, farmhouses for hus-
> bandmen, which are well contrived, and are furnished with all
> things necessary for country labor." [4]

In Bellamy's ideal society farm land is publicly owned
and operated, although:

> Every one, of course, has his own house and piece of land if
> he or she desires them ... but these are allotments for use only,
> and, being always equal, can furnish no ground for dissension. [5]

PUBLIC WORK AND LABOR ROTATION

Both More and Bellamy follow Peru in providing for
public work and for rotation of labor on the land and elsewhere. According to Prescott:

> By this constant rotation of labour it was intended that no one
> should be overburdened, and that each man should have time
> to provide for the demands of his own household. It was impos-
> sible—in the judgment of a high Spanish authority—to improve
> on the system of distribution, so carefully was it accommodated
> to the condition and comfort of the artisan. [6]

Means discusses the same subject:

> Every craftsman who labored in the service of the Inca
> or of his Curaca [local supervisor] must be provided with all
> the raw materials for his labor, so that his contribution consisted
> only of his time, work, and dexterity. His employment in this
> way was not to be more than two or three months in the year.
> [That is not a much greater portion of the year's work than an
> American contributes to his government through taxes.]
> A craftsman was to be supplied with food, clothes, and medi-
> cine at need while he was working. ...

The surplus of the tribute, after the royal wants had been satisfied, were placed on deposit and drawn upon for the good of the people as required.

In special cases tribute was paid in the form of work upon the roads, upon the temples, palaces, aqueducts, bridges, storehouses, or other public works. In other cases the tribute-payers were called upon to serve as *chasqui-cuna* (post runners) or as litter-bearers or as miners.

"...each man had very light work, because their turns were regulated with great exactness, and one never had more to do than another." [Father Blas Valera] I think my readers will agree with me that the world has never seen a code of laws more exquisitely logical nor more sublimely just.[7]

The description of labor rotation in More's *Utopia* is as follows:

Inhabitants are sent by turns from the cities to dwell in [the houses built for farmers]...Every year twenty of this family come back to the town, after they have stayed two years in the country; and in their room there are other twenty sent from the town, that they may learn country work from those that have been already one year in the country, as they must teach those that come to them the next from the town. By this means such as dwell in those country farms are never ignorant of agriculture... But though there is every year such a shifting of the husbandmen, to prevent any man being forced against his will to follow that hard course of life too long; yet many among them take such pleasure in it, that they desire leave to continue in it many years.[8]

Bellamy's program, though less regimented, and more flexible, is to the same effect. Referring in *Equality* to "the isolation, the loneliness, the lack of social intercourse and opportunity of social culture which were incident to the farmer's life" under the old regime, he says of the citizen under the new order:

"He, like the others, lives where he pleases ... Work on a farm no longer implies life on a farm, unless for those who like it ... It is not uncommon on a few days' notice to throw a hundred thousand extra workers into a region where there is a special temporary demand for [farm] labor." [9]

CENSUS AND INVENTORY

In order for the Inca to plan production and to apportion distribution it was necessary to have a periodical census and inventory. In this respect, too, both More and Bellamy follow the Peruvian practice. According to Prescott, the Incas had achieved statistical records of production and consumption which were far beyond those of any European or Asiatic government. He says:

The nature and amount of the services required were all determined at Cuzco [the capital of the empire] by commissioners well instructed in the resources of the country and in the character of the inhabitants of different provinces.

This information was obtained by an admirable regulation, which has scarcely a counterpart in the annals of a semi-civilised people. A register was kept of all the births and deaths throughout the country, and exact returns of the actual population were made to the government every year ... At certain intervals, also, a general survey of the country was made, exhibiting a complete view of the character of the soil, its fertility, the nature of its products, both agricultural and mineral,—in short, of all that constituted the physical resources of the empire. Furnished with these statistical details, it was easy for the government, after determining the amount of requisitions, to distribute the work among the respective provinces best qualified to execute it.

An inventory of the various products of the country, and the quarters whence they were obtained, was every year taken by the royal officers, and recorded by the *quipu-camayus* on their registers, with surprising regularity and precision. These registers were transmitted to the capital and submitted to the Inca, who could thus at a glance, as it were, embrace the whole results of the national industry and see how far they corresponded with the requisitions of the government.

The quantity of the cloth needed, as well as the peculiar kind and quality of the fabric, was first determined at Cuzco. The work was then apportioned among the different provinces. Officers appointed for the purpose superintended the distribution of the wool, so that the manufacture of the different articles should be intrusted to the most competent hands.

The like course was pursued with reference to the other requisitions of the government ... the labour of a larger number of hands was exacted for the execution of the great public works which covered the land.[10]

Means refers to:

... the system of statistics which provided the ruler with exact information concerning the material wealth, the value, existent in each district, and also concerning the man-power therein ... The Incas had to depend upon the *quipu* for the preservation of their records. ... By means of the *quipu* the *quipu-camayoc*, knot-record keeper, could enumerate and calculate in the decimal system. In this respect the Incas were far ahead of the Romans, with their clumsy system of figures, and even of the modern British, with their absurd £.s.d.... "These [quipus] were long ropes made of knotted cords, and those who were accountants and understood the arrangement of these knots, could, by their means, give an account of the expenditure, and of other things during a long course of years." [Cieza][11]

More's *Utopia* covers this subject as follows:

In their great council at Amaurot [Cuzco of Peru?], to which there are three sent from every town once a year, they examine what towns abound in provisions, and what are under any scarcity, that so the one may be furnished from the other; and this is done freely, without any sort of exchange; for according to their plenty or scarcity, they supply, or are supplied from one another; so that indeed the whole island is, as it were, one family. When they have thus taken care of their whole country, and laid up stores for two years, which they do to prevent the ill consequences of an unfavorable season, they order an exportation of the over-plus ... [12]

In *Looking Backward* we find provision for similar statistical controls.

SYSTEM OF STOREHOUSES

In the direct economy of ancient Peru, wealth did not consist of stocks and bonds or tokens, but of things themselves and of improved lands and production facilities. To smooth out irregularities of nature and men, a system of storehouses was necessary. Prescott makes several references to this remarkable system:

At the appointed season they [the llamas in the public flocks] were well sheared, and the wool was deposited in the public magazines.

A part of the agricultural produce and manufactures was transported to Cuzco, to minister to the immediate demands of the Inca and his court. But far the greater part was stored in magazines scattered over the different provinces. These spacious buildings, constructed of stone, were divided between the Sun and the Inca, though the greater share seems to have been appropriated by the monarch. By a wise regulation, any deficiency in the contributions of the Inca might be supplied from the granaries of the Sun. But such a necessity could rarely have happened; and the providence of the government usually left a large surplus in the royal depositories, which was removed to a third class of magazines, whose design was to supply the people in seasons of scarcity, and, occasionally, to furnish relief to individuals whom sickness or misfortune had reduced to poverty; thus in a manner justifying the assertion of a Castilian document, that a large portion of the revenues of the Inca found its way back again, through one channel or another, into the hands of the people. These magazines were found by the Spaniards, on their arrival, stored with all the various products and manufactures of the country,—with maize, *coca quinua*, woollen and cotton stuffs of the finest quality, with vases and utensils of gold, silver and copper, in short, with every article of luxury or use within the compass of Peruvian skill. The magazines of grain, in particular, would frequently have sufficed for the consumption of the adjoining district for several years.[13]

The description in *Utopia* is brief, but specific:

Every city is divided into four equal parts, and in the middle of each there is a market place: what is brought thither, and manufactured by the several families, is carried from thence to houses appointed for that purpose, in which all things of a sort are laid by themselves . . . [14]

In *Looking Backward* we find similar provisions:

"All our [retail] stores are sample stores, except as to a few classes of articles. The goods, with these exceptions, are all at the great central warehouse of the city, to which they are shipped directly from the producers. We order from the sample . . . The orders are sent to the warehouse, and the goods distributed from there." [15]

A MONEYLESS ECONOMY

An economy without money, and without buying or selling except for local exchange of surplus local goods, seems strange to Europeans or Americans, but the great Peruvian empire throve on such a system. Means gives his judgment of the nature of their commerce:

The commerce of the nation, as I see it in the light of the evidence adduced, was chiefly a local matter conducted under governmental supervision at the various grades of fairs or markets, supplemented by long-distance traffic which was wholly in the hands of the imperial authorities.[16]

He indicates further:

...they were able to build public works which no modern society, always governed in its enterprises by the monetary factor, could hope to accomplish in those regions with financial profit... By means of these beneficial public works the Incas increased the yield of their realm tremendously and built up for themselves a renown which has never faded away.[17]

According to Prescott:

Under this extraordinary polity, a people advanced in many of the social refinements, well skilled in manufactures and agriculture, were unacquainted, as we have seen, with money. They had nothing that deserved to be called property.[18]

The account in *Utopia* has a strangely similar sound. Not only did More speak of this moneyless economy as being "the foundation of all the rest," but he went into details:

...they [the Utopians] sow much more, and breed more cattle than are necessary for their consumption; and they give that overplus of which they make no use to their neighbors. When they want anything in the country which it does not produce, they fetch that from the town, without carrying anything in exchange for it.

...there being no property among them, every man may freely enter into any house whatsoever.

...every father goes and takes whatsoever he or his family stand in need of, without either paying for it, or leaving anything in exchange.

In all other places it is visible, that while people talk of a commonwealth, every man only seeks his own wealth; but there, where no man has any property, all men zealously pursue the good of the public; and, indeed, it is no wonder to see men act so differently; for in other commonwealths every man knows that unless he provides for himself, how flourishing soever the commonwealth may be, he must die of hunger; so that he sees the necessity of preferring his own concerns to the public; but in Utopia, where every man has a right to everything, they all know that if care is taken to keep the public stores full, no private man can want anything ...[19]

Bellamy, too, outlines an identical moneyless state:

"... as soon as the nation became the sole producer of all sorts of commodities, there was no need of exchanges between individuals that they might get what they required. Everything was procurable from one source, and nothing could be procured anywhere else. A system of direct distribution from the national storehouses took the place of trade, and for this money was unnecessary." [20]

ORGANIZATION OF THE POPULATION

For this moneyless economy to be successful, it was necessary that all those able to do so should work. According to Markham and to Means, the entire Inca population was divided into ten classes, from infancy to old age.* The first five classes, from birth to sixteen years old, were not required to work. From sixteen to twenty they did light manual work, such as coca picking, and from twenty to twenty-five they helped their elders at their tasks. The *puric*, or able-bodied man from twenty-five to fifty, was head of a house-

---

* Robert Owen's utopian writings, dating from twenty years before Prescott's *Conquest of Peru*, also recapitulated Peruvian economy in important respects. In his classification of the population into age groups, he went further in the direction of Peru than did Thomas More. Where, except in *Utopia*, did he find his pattern? Various descriptions of Peruvian economy translated into English were accessible to him.

hold and payer of tribute; from fifty to sixty he was "half old," doing light work; the tenth grade, that of *puñuc-rucu*, or "old men sleeping," made up of those beyond sixty, were free from work.[21]

More covers the same ground in *Utopia:*

. . . in a great city, and in all the territory that lies round it, you can scarce find five hundred, either men or women, [who] by their age and strength, are capable of labor, that are not engaged in it; even the Syphogrants, though excused by the law, yet do not excuse themselves, but work, that by their examples they may incite the industry of the rest of the people.[22]

On the matter of universal obligation to work, Bellamy leaves no doubt whatsoever:

". . . to speak of service being compulsory would be a weak way to state its absolute inevitableness. Our entire social order is so wholly based upon and deduced from it that if it were conceivable that a man could escape it, he would be left with no possible way to provide for his existence." [23]

SUPERVISION OF LABOR

This universal labor required a program of supervision, and this, too, is common to Peru, *Utopia*, and *Looking Backward*. Prescott describes the process:

The task of apportioning the labour was assigned to the local authorities, and great care was taken that it should be done in such a manner that, while the most competent hands were selected, the weight should not fall disproportionately on any.

The people were not allowed to be employed on works pernicious to their health, nor to pine—a sad contrast to their subsequent destiny—under the imposition of tasks too heavy for their powers. They were never made the victims of public or private extortions; and a benevolent forecast watched carefully over their necessities, and provided for their relief in seasons of infirmity and for their sustenance in health. The government of the Incas, however arbitrary in form, was in its spirit truly patriarchal.[24]

Utopia provides similarly for labor supervision:

The chief, and almost the only business of the syphogrants, is to take care that no man may live idle, but that every one may follow his trade diligently; yet they do not wear themselves out with perpetual toil, from morning to night, as if they were beasts of burden...[25]

The idea of supervision of labor runs through Bellamy's two books, *Looking Backward* and *Equality*, and no brief quotation is adequate. The following from *Looking Backward* is an example of the genius of Bellamy in realizing the greatest degree of regulation with the least degree of regimentation:

"It is the business of the administration to seek constantly to equalize the attractions of the trades...This is done by making the hours of labor in different trades to differ according to their arduousness. The lighter trades, prosecuted under the most agreeable circumstances, have in this way the longest hours, while an arduous trade, such as mining, has very short hours.... The administration ... simply follows the fluctuations of opinion among the workers themselves as indicated by the rate of volunteering. The principle is that no man's work ought to be, on the whole, harder for him than any other man's for him, the workers themselves to be the judges...." [26]

The problem of supervision of the "industrial army" is a major issue with Bellamy, and on the whole was skillfully handled.

HOURS OF WORK

This vast program made possible limitations of hours of work. Prescott says:

... no one was required to give more than a stipulated portion of his time to the public service. He was then succeeded by another for the like term; and it should be observed that all who were engaged in the employment of the government—and the remark applies equally to agricultural labour—were maintained, for the time, at the public expense.

The security of the working-classes seems to have been ever kept in view in the regulations of the government; and these were so discreetly arranged that the most wearing and unwholesome labours, as those of the mines, occasioned no detriment to the health of the labourer; a striking contract to his subsequent condition under which the Spanish rule.[27]

The story is repeated in *Utopia:*

... it frequently happens, that for want of other work, vast numbers are sent out to mend the highways. But when no public undertaking is to be performed, the hours of working are lessened. The magistrates never engage the people in unnecessary labor, since the chief end of the constitution is to regulate labor by the necessities of the public, and to allow all the people as much time as is necessary for the improvement of their minds, in which they think the happiness of life consists.

... they, dividing the day and night into twenty-four hours, appoint six of these for work; three of which are before dinner; and three after.[28]

With technological developments pictured in *Looking Backward,* Bellamy could forecast even shorter working hours.

DIGNITY OF LABOR

Labor was honorable in Peru. Means, in his *Ancient Civilizations of the Andes,* emphasizes this principle:

The dignified position held by manual labor in the Incaic polity is made apparent by the fact that everyone, from the Inca downwards, participated in it ... Garcilaso ... tells us that ... the terrace called Collcampata ... "was cultivated by persons of the blood royal, and none but Incas and Pallas (Ladies) could work on it." [29]

So it was also in *Utopia:*

... if there is anywhere a rough, hard, and sordid piece of work to be done ... they cheerfully, and of their own accord, take that to their share ... but by their stooping to such servile employments, they are so far from being despised, that they are so much the more esteemed by the whole nation. [30]

With this attitude Bellamy is in complete accord:

". . . it is an axiom of ethics that to accept a service from another which we would be unwilling to return in kind, if need were, is like borrowing with the intention of not repaying, while to enforce such a service by taking advantage of the poverty or necessity of a person would be an outrage like forcible robbery. It is the worst thing about any system which divides men, or allows them to be divided, into classes and castes, that it weakens the sense of a common humanity.

". . . there is recognized no sort of difference between the dignity of the different sorts of work required by the nation." [31]

TRADES AND HANDICRAFTS

In the matter of handicrafts, Prescott relates:

The natives showed a skill in other mechanical arts similar to that displayed by their manufactures of cloth. Every man in Peru was expected to be acquainted with the various handicrafts essential to domestic comfort.

... the wool was deposited in the public magazines. It was then dealt out to each family in such quantities as sufficed for its wants, and was consigned to the female part of the household, who were well instructed in the business of spinning and weaving.[32]

On the same point More says of "Utopia":

... every man has some peculiar trade to which he applies himself, such as the manufacture of wool, or flax, masonry, smith's work, or carpenter's work ... Every family makes their own clothes; but all among them, women as well as men, learn one or other of the trades formerly mentioned. Women, for the most part, deal in wool and flax, which suit best with their weakness, leaving the ruder trades to the men.[33]

In each case these callings were hereditary. Prescott says:

The different provinces of the country furnished persons peculiarly suited to different employments, which, as we shall see hereafter, usually descended from father to son.[34]

More in *Utopia* treats of the same point as follows:

The same trade generally passes down from father to son, inclinations often following descent; but if any man's genius lies another way, he is by adoption translated into a family that deals in the trade to which he is inclined ...[35]

AN ECONOMY OF ABUNDANCE

The effect of the Peruvian economy was a universal abundance, on the very simple scale of living which prevailed. Growing out of that equality and security there is pictured a fading away of greed and avarice. According to Prescott:

No man could be rich, no man could be poor, in Peru; but all might enjoy, and did enjoy, a competence. Ambition, avarice, the love of change, the morbid spirit of discontent, those passions which most agitate the minds of men, found no place in the bosom of the Peruvian.[36]

Means, in his *Fall of the Inca Empire,* supports this view. He says:

The empire ruled by this most rational of systems was one whose people were as fortunate, in a material way at least, as any who have ever lived. If laws were severe, the people suffered but little from that severity because the laws were seldom flouted; if all, high and low, had to work in appropriate manners for the good of the state, all alike received recompense in the form of security against want of all kinds. Money was unknown, and so also were the myriad evils—avarice, corruption, cruelty, and oppression—which follow in its train ...[37]

It would seem that More was describing this economy when he wrote in *Utopia:*

... among them there is no unequal distribution, so that no man is poor, none in necessity; and though no man has anything, yet they are all rich; for what can make a man so rich as to lead a serene and cheerful life, free from anxieties ...

There is no reason for giving a denial to any person, since there is such plenty of everything among them; and there is no danger of a man's asking for more than he needs; they have no inducements to do this, since they are sure that they shall always be supplied. It is the fear of want that makes any of the whole race of animals either greedy or ravenous; but besides fear, there is in a man a pride that makes him fancy it a particular glory to excel others in pomp and excess. But by the laws of the Utopians there is no room for this.

... the use as well as the desire of money being extinguished, much anxiety and great occasions of mischief are cut off with them. And who does not see that the frauds, thefts, robberies, quarrels, tumults, contentions, seditions, murders, treacheries, and witchcrafts, which are indeed rather punished than restrained by the severities of law, would all fall off, if money were not any more valued by the world? Men's fears, solicitudes, cares, labors, and watchings would all perish in the same moment with the value of money: even poverty itself, for the relief of which money seems most necessary, would fall.[38]

The entire program of Bellamy is based upon the feasibility of an economy of abundance. As a typical expression, he wrote in *Looking Backward*:

"No man any more has any care for the morrow, either for himself or his children, for the nation guarantees the nurture, education, and comfortable maintenance of every citizen from the cradle to the grave.[39]

With modern labor-saving technology, that seems a far more reasonable forecast than did the prophecy of More in his day, and it would be far less like a miracle than the actual achievement of the Incas. Bellamy also believed that absence of acute want would reduce the tendency to crime. He says:

"Directly or indirectly, the desire for money, which then meant every good thing, was the motive of all this crime, the taproot of a vast poison growth ... When we made the nation the sole trustee of the wealth of the people, and guaranteed to all abundant maintenance, on the one hand abolishing want, and on the other checking the accumulation of riches, we cut this root, and the poison tree that overshadowed your society withered ..." [40]

AGRICULTURE

With regard to agriculture there is a very striking degree of similarity between Peru and *Utopia*, and to some extent between these and *Looking Backward*. A description of Inca agriculture is interesting in that it shows clearly that the universal well-being which the country enjoyed was not due to prodigal favors of nature, but was largely won from barren deserts and steep rugged mountains by wise planning and highly efficient administration of vast public works. It is striking evidence of the practical effectiveness of the kind of social economy described by More and Bellamy, and as practiced in Peru. Prescott's description of how natural difficulties were overcome is impressive:

The face of the country would appear to be peculiarly unfavourable to the purposes both of agriculture and of internal communication. The sandy strip along the coast, where rain rarely falls, is fed only by a few scanty streams . . . The precipitous steeps of the sierra, with its splintered sides of porphyry and granite, and its higher regions wrapped in snows that never melt . . . might seem equally unpropitious to the labours of the husbandman.

The soil, it is true, was for the most part sandy and sterile; but many places . . . needed only to be properly irrigated to be susceptible of extraordinary production. To these spots water was conveyed by means of canals and subterraneous aqueducts executed on a noble scale. . . . Some of these aqueducts were of great length. One . . . measured between four and five hundred miles. . . . In this descent a passage was sometimes to be opened through rocks,— and this without the aid of iron tools; impracticable mountains were to be turned, rivers and marshes to be crossed; in short, the same obstacles were to be encountered as in the construction of their mighty roads.

Many of the hills, though covered with a strong soil, were too precipitous to be tilled. These they cut into terraces, faced with rough stone, diminishing in regular gradation towards the summit; so that, while the lower strip, or *anden*, as it was called by the Spaniards, that belted round the base of the mountain, might comprehend hundreds of acres, the uppermost was only large enough to accommodate a few rows of Indian corn. . . . With such patient toil did the Peruvians combat the formidable obstacles presented by the face of their country! Without the use of the tools or the machinery familiar to the European, each individual could have done little; but acting in large masses, and under a common direction, they were enabled by indefatigable perseverance to achieve results to have attempted which might have filled even the European with dismay.

In the same spirit of economical husbandry which redeemed the rocky sierra from the curse of sterility, they dug below the arid soil of the valleys and sought for a stratum where some natural moisture might be found. These excavations, called by the Spaniards *hoyas,* or "pits," were made on a great scale, comprehending frequently more than an acre, sunk to the depth of fifteen or twenty feet, and fenced round within by a wall of *adobes,* or bricks baked in the sun. The bottom of the excavation, well prepared by a rich manure of the sardines,—a small fish obtained in vast quantities along the coast,—was planted with some kind of grain or vegetable.

Under their patient and discriminating culture, every inch of good soil was tasked to its greatest power of production; while the most unpromising spots were compelled to contribute something to the subsistence of the people. Everywhere the land teemed with evidence of agricultural wealth, from the smiling valleys along the coast to the terraced steeps of the sierra, which, rising into pyramids of verdure, glowed with all the splendours of tropical vegetation.[41]

In comparison with these great works, how limited is agricultural mastery of our own broad, fertile, and well-watered acres, aided as it is by steam, electricity, modern machinery, high explosives, and universal transportation and communication. The security and contentment of the Peruvian farmer presents a striking contrast to the insecurity of American agriculture. Here the mortgage hangs over the farm like the sword of Damocles, or the tenant shifts from farm to farm in restless, poverty-bound discontent, or the migrant farm worker roams in near hopelessness from farm to farm and from crop to crop. It would seem that a money economy is not the only way to administer agriculture.

More's *Utopia* in total is but a short essay, and his information at best must have been very incomplete; consequently most subjects are treated briefly. Yet what he does say concerning agriculture is in harmony with Prescott:

... though they ... have neither the most fruitful soil nor the purest air in the world, yet ... by their industry they so cultivate their soil, that there is nowhere to be seen a greater increase both of corn and cattle, nor are there anywhere healthier men, and freer from diseases: for one may there see reduced to practice ... all the art that the husbandman employs in manuring and improving an ill soil ...

They cultivate their gardens with great care, so that they have both vines, fruits, herbs, and flowers in them; and all is so well ordered, and so finely kept, that I never saw gardens anywhere that were both so fruitful and so beautiful as theirs.[42]

Both in Peru and in Utopia, everyone, except the small ruling class, was in agriculture. As this was a condition unknown in Europe or Asia, and is not necessary to the economy described in *Utopia*, the likeness is all the more remarkable. Prescott states:

Every Peruvian of the lower class was a husbandman, and, with the exception of those already specified, was expected to provide for his own support by the cultivation of his land.

Husbandry was pursued by them on principles that may be truly called scientific. It was the basis of their political institutions. Having no foreign commerce, it was agriculture that furnished them with the means of their internal exchanges, their subsistence, and their revenues. We have seen their remarkable provisions for distributing the land in equal shares among the people, while they required every man, except the privileged orders, to assist in its cultivation. The Inca himself did not disdain to set the example. [Later students of Peru are of the opinion that foreign commerce was not entirely lacking.] [43]

Thomas More, in his brief way, covers the same ground:

Agriculture is that which is so universally understood among them, that no person, either man or woman, is ignorant of it; they are instructed in it from their childhood, partly by what they learn at school, and partly by practice; they being led out often into the fields, about the town, where they not only see others at work, but are likewise exercised in it themselves.[44]

In one respect the Peruvian system had a simplicity and economy which is not envisaged in *Looking Backward*. Since each family raised the greater part of its own food and made most of its own clothes, the national economic system was relieved of the great bulk of the burden of administration and of distribution. Even in a present-day technological economy, a decentralization of population and of industry which would allow a higher degree of local self-support would greatly disencumber and simplify the economic process. In fact, such a decentralization of production as that of Peru may be a necessary condition to the effective working of such a state as that described in *Utopia* or in *Looking Backward*. Bellamy missed this point in his first utopia, but in its sequel, *Equality*, he corrected that oversight. America, whether under a money economy as at present, or under a direct service economy as pictured by Bellamy, might go far toward achieving stability, eliminating waste motion, and reducing want, by realizing more of the possibilities of local and regional self-sufficiency.

FAMILY GROUPS

The fundamental social organization described in *Utopia* is very similar to that outlined by Means in his *Ancient Civilizations of the Andes*. In Utopia "no country family has fewer than forty men and women in it, besides two slaves," governed by a master and a mistress; whereas in the Peruvian society, though chronicles differ somewhat, it seems clear that there were officials in charge of ten households. In Utopia there was an official over each thirty families. In Peru, according to Means, there were officials in charge of fifty households. In the Peruvian economy there was an ascending scale of family groups with officials in charge of one hundred, five hundred, one thousand, ten thousand, and forty thousand families, with finally four officials, each in charge of a quarter of the empire, with the Inca at the head. What a wonderful training school for administrators this system provided!

COLONIZATION

The Inca habit of adjusting the population to regional resources by colonization is closely approximated in *Utopia*. Means quotes Garcilaso, the greatest of all Peruvian historians, whose mother was an Inca princess:

"In the course of their conquests the Incas found some provinces to be naturally fertile, but thinly populated. To these districts they sent Indians who were natives of other provinces with a similar climate. . . . When the inhabitants of a locality multiplied rapidly, so that their province was not large enough to hold them, they removed a certain proportion of the people to some other district. They also removed Indians from barren and sterile tracts to such as were fertile and prolific. . . . Colonists were also sent to other provinces for a reason of state. . . ." [45]

In *Utopia* we read:

. . . they supply cities that do not increase so fast, from others that breed faster; and if there is any increase over the whole island, then they draw out a number of their citizens out of the several towns, and send them over to the neighboring continent; where, if they find that the inhabitants have more soil than they can well cultivate, they fix a colony, taking the inhabitants into their society, if they are willing to live with them . . . [46]

FEW LAWS

In each case there were few laws. As Prescott states:

The laws were few and exceedingly severe. They related almost wholly to criminal matters. Few other laws were needed by a people who had no money, little trade, and hardly anything that could be called fixed property.

... in a country like Peru, where few but criminal causes were known, the right of appeal was of less consequence. The law was simple, its application easy; and, where the judge was honest, the case was as likely to be determined correctly on the first hearing as on the second.... The law which required a decision within five days would seem little suited to the complex and embarrassing litigation of a modern tribunal. But... the Spaniards, familiar with the evils growing out of long-protracted suits, where the successful litigant is too often a ruined man, are loud in their encomiums of this swift-handed and economical justice.[47]

In *Utopia* we find the following: "They have but few laws, and such is their constitution that they need not many."

Here Bellamy is in agreement:

"With no private property to speak of, no disputes between citizens over business relations, no real estate to divide or debts to collect, there must be absolutely no civil business at all for them; and with no offenses against property, and mighty few of any sort to provide criminal cases, I should think you might almost do without judges and lawyers altogether."

"We do without the lawyers, certainly," was Dr. Leete's reply.

"There is neither private property, beyond personal belongings, now, nor buying and selling, and therefore the occasion of nearly all the legislation formerly necessary has passed away." [48]

III

Non–Utopian Parallels

COMPARISONS OF SOCIAL AND ECONOMIC organization do not exhaust likenesses between Peru on the one hand and More's *Utopia* on the other. From some of the "un-utopian" aspects of his society there is also evidence that More may have received many of his ideas from a report on the land of the Incas.

There is a price to pay for this high level of economic well-being, and here both More and Bellamy are in partial agreement with the economy of Peru. Prescott writes of the Peruvians, not including the small royal class of officials and priests:

They could follow no craft, could engage in no labour, no amusement, but such as was specially provided by law. They could not change their residence or their dress without a license from the government. They could not even exercise the freedom which is conceded to the most abject in other countries,—that of selecting their own wives.

The astonishing mechanism of the Peruvian polity could have resulted only from the combined authority of opinion and positive power in the ruler to an extent unprecedented in the history of man. Yet that it should have so successfully gone into operation, and so long endured, in opposition to the taste, the prejudices, and the very principles of our nature, is a strong proof of a generally wise and temperate administration of the government.[1]

Even these are not the harshest words which Prescott used in describing a social order so different from that of his home state of Massachusetts.

More's picture of Utopia also includes much of regimentation:

> If any man has a mind to visit his friends that live in some other town, or desires to travel and see the rest of the country, he obtains leave very easily from the Syphogrant and Tranibors, when there is no particular occasion for him at home. Such as travel, carry with them a passport from the Prince, which both certifies the license that is granted for traveling, and limits the time of their return ... if any man goes out of the city to which he belongs, without leave, and is found rambling without a passport, he is severely treated, he is punished as a fugitive, and sent home disgracefully; and if he falls again into the like fault, is condemned to slavery. ... all men live in full view, so that all are obliged, both to perform their ordinary task and to employ themselves well in their spare hours.[2]

R. W. Chambers, in his scholarly and eulogistic life of Thomas More, emphasizes, apparently with approval, this element of personal subordination in *Utopia*. He says, "... the ideal of *Utopia* is discipline, not liberty. It is influenced by some of the most severe disciplines the world has ever known."[3] Again he says of More, "He had been the first modern to draw a picture of the corporate state with its remorseless discipline. In *Utopia* he had reserved to the individual almost nothing, save the integrity of his soul ..."[4] In another place he says, "If the Utopian attempts to break the laws of his native land, there is the penalty of bondage, and behind that of death. Even to speak of state affairs, except at the licensed place and hour, is punishable in Utopia with death, lest permission to discuss politics might lead to revolution. Has any State, at any time, carried terrorism quite so far?" [5]

Another of Thomas More's admirers and defenders supports the view that there would be small liberty in Utopia. In *More's Utopia and His Social Teaching*, William Edward Campbell writes:

The first general impression that comes to us of the Utopian life is that it was one of very severe discipline. Everything is made subservient to the general good, and few of the inhabitants of Utopia rejoice even in a small measure of personal independence.

Each individual Utopian was but a pawn in the hand of the governing powers. A twentieth-century individual prides himself upon his freedom to go wherever he pleases and whenever it pleases him. But in Utopia a man could hardly move more than a few hundred yards without an official leave to do so. Nor, again, could he stay where he was for very long without special permission.[6]

In this respect Campbell's appraisal of *Utopia* corresponds to Prescott's opinion of Peru.

Under the pleasant language we see also the element of regimentation in Bellamy's program:

"... but a worker may likewise, under suitable regulations and not too frequently, obtain a transfer to an establishment of the same industry in another part of the country which for any reason he may prefer ... It is only the poorest sort of workmen who desire to change even as frequently as our regulations permit." [7]

Miss Emily Balch, the sociologist, writes that when her father read *Looking Backward* at the time of its first publication, he said, "It is slavery, but it's worth it." Bellamy sought to keep open the possibilities of spontaneity and initiative. He was willing to give up some liberty for privileged men in order to insure a degree of economic freedom for all men. He seems to have borrowed from Peru, but did not blindly imitate.

Various writers have wondered why Thomas More, in writing of an ideal commonwealth, should have included some elements that are sordid, brutal, and unideal. For instance, Lewis Mumford, in his *The Story of Utopias*, says:

The greater part of the business of the government [of Utopia] relates to the economic life of the people. There are certain other matters, however, which remain over for them; and these affairs constitute a blot on More's conception of the ideal commonwealth. One of them is the regulation of travel; another is the treatment of crime; and a third is war.

While any man may travel if there is no particular occasion for him at home—whether he wishes to visit friends or see the rest of the country—it is necessary for him to carry a passport from the Prince. If he stay in any place longer than a night he must follow his proper occupation; and if anyone goes out of the city without leave or is found wandering around without a passport, he is punished as a fugitive, and upon committing the offense a second time is condemned to slavery. This is a plain example of unimaginative harshness; and it is hard to explain away; indeed, I have no intention to.

Apparently More could not conceive of a perfectly happy commonwealth for the majority of men if they still had to perform certain filthy daily tasks, like the slaughtering of beef; and so he attempts to kill two birds with one stone; he creates a class of slaves, and he fills this class by condemning to it people who have committed venial crimes. In doing this, he overlooks the final objection to slavery in all its forms; namely, that it tends to corrupt the master.

Since we are discussing the conditions that undermine More's commonwealth, we may remark that war, too, remains; the difference being that the Utopians attempt to do by strategy, corruption, and what we should now call propaganda, what less intelligent people do by sheer force of arms.... Among the just causes of war the Utopians count the seizure of territory, the oppression of foreign merchants, and the denial of access to land to nations capable of cultivating it. They take considerable pains to keep their "best sort of men for their own use at home, so they make use of the worst sort of men for the consumption of war." [8]

It is very interesting to note that every single particular of Utopia mentioned by Mumford as inappropriate to an ideal commonwealth, is descriptive of Peru. Even the peculiar detail that slaves were required to do the butchering corresponds to facts in Peru, in that almost the principal use of slaves, who were descendants of military captives, was to serve in the temples, where many animals were slaughtered as sacrifices. Hunting for sport was outlawed in Peru. Compare all this with More in *Utopia:* "Therefore all this exercise of hunting, as a thing unworthy to be used of free men, the Utopians have rejected to their butchers; to the which craft, as we said before, they appoint their bondmen." Is it not probable that in including these unideal elements More simply was describing the land of the Incas as Hythloday had described it? In that light it is not "hard to explain away."

The peculiar methods by which the Peruvians waged war had little to do with the economic system, and were far from ideal; yet More includes them with great accuracy in his *Utopia.* Prescott, in describing the military campaigns of the Incas, and in comparing Inca and Aztec practices, says:

Very different was the policy pursued by the two races in their military career. The Aztecs, animated by the most ferocious spirit, carried on a war of extermination, signalizing their triumphs by the sacrifice of hecatombs of captives; while the Incas, although they pursued the game of conquest with equal pertinacity, preferred a milder policy, substituting negotiation and intrigue for violence, and dealt with their antagonists so that their future resources should not be crippled, and that they should come as friends, not as foes, into the bosom of the empire.

In every stage of the war, he [the Inca] was open to propositions for peace; and, although he sought to reduce his enemies by carrying off their harvests and distressing them by famine, he allowed his troops to commit no unnecessary outrage on person or property. "We must spare our enemies," one of the Peruvian princes is quoted as saying, "or it will be our loss, since they and all that belongs to them must soon be ours."

They sought to soften the hearts of the rude tribes around them, and melt them by acts of condescension and kindness. Far from provoking hostilities, they allowed time for the salutary example of their own institutions to work its effect, trusting that their less civilized neighbours would submit to their sceptre, from a conviction of the blessings it would secure to them. When this course failed, they employed other measures, but still of a pacific character, and endeavoured by negotiation, by conciliatory treatment, and by presents to the leading men, to win them over to their dominion. In short, they practised all the arts familiar to the most subtle politician of a civilized land to secure the acquisition of empire. When all these expedients failed, they prepared for war.[9]

Means supports this view. He says:

Garcilaso repeatedly makes it clear that conquered chiefs who finally submitted with good grace, and chiefs of states who came into the empire without resisting the Inca, were continued in office and were fitted into the hierarchy of the Incaic administration, each one taking a rank therein to which his position prior to conquest entitled him. Only contumacious chiefs were cast down and replaced by others of the Inca's appointment or of his viceroy's appointment.[10]

Note how closely More follows this description:

They would be both troubled and ashamed of a bloody victory over their enemies, and think it would be as foolish a purchase as to buy the most valuable goods at too high a rate. And in no victory do they glory so much as in that which is gained by dexterity and good conduct, without bloodshed.

They very much approve of this way of corrupting their enemies, though it appears to others to be base and cruel; but they look on it as a wise course, to make an end of what would be otherwise a long war, without so much as hazarding one battle to decide it.

If this method does not succeed with them, then they sow seeds of contention among their enemies, and animate the prince's brother, or some of the nobility, to aspire to the crown. If they cannot disunite them by domestic broils, then they engage their neighbors against them, and make them set on foot some old pretensions, which are never wanting to princes when they have occasion for them.[11]

Also, in treatment of conquered peoples we see similar likenesses. According to Prescott:

Their policy towards the conquered forms a contrast no less striking to that pursued by the Aztecs. The Mexican vassals were ground by excessive imposts and military conscriptions. No regard was had to their welfare, and the only limit to oppression was the power of endurance.... [They] were made to feel every hour that they were not part and parcel of the nation, but held only in subjugation as a conquered people. The Incas, on the other hand, admitted their new subjects at once to all the rights enjoyed by the rest of the community and though they made them conform to the established laws and usages of the empire, they watched over their personal security and comfort with a sort of parental solicitude. The motley population, thus bound together by common interest, was animated by a common feeling of loyalty, which gave greater strength and stability to the empire as it became more and more widely extended... The policy of the two nations displayed the principle of fear as contrasted with the principle of love.[12]

More in *Utopia* treats of the same subject:

They never lay their enemies' country waste, nor burn their corn, and even in their marches they take all possible care that neither horse nor foot may tread it down, for they do not know but that they may have use for it themselves. They hurt no man whom they find disarmed, unless he is a spy. When a town is surrendered to them, they take it into their protection: and when they carry a place by storm, they never plunder it, but put those only to the sword that opposed the rendering of it up, and make the rest of the garrison slaves, but for the other inhabitants they do them no hurt; and if any of them had advised a surrender, they give them good rewards out of the estates of those that they condemn, and distribute the rest among their auxiliary troops, but they themselves take no share of the spoil.[13]

The comments on a common language are strikingly similar. Prescott says of Peru:

It was determined ... to substitute [for regional dialects] one universal language, the *Quichua*,—the language of the court, the capital, and the surrounding country,—the richest and most comprehensive of the South American dialects. Teachers were provided in the towns and villages throughout the land, who were to give instruction to all, even the humblest classes; and it was intimated at the same time that no one should be raised to any office of dignity or profit who was unacquainted with this tongue. . . . while each province retained its peculiar tongue, a beautiful medium of communication was introduced, which enabled the inhabitants of one part of the country to hold intercourse with every other, and the Inca and his deputies to communicate with all. This was the state of things on the arrival of the Spaniards.

Thus naturalized in the remotest provinces, it became enriched by a variety of exotic words and idioms, which, under the influence of the court and of poetic culture, if I may so express myself, was gradually blended, like some finished mosaic made up of coarse and disjointed materials, into one harmonious whole.[14]

More is briefer in his comment:

They have all their learning in their own tongue, which is both a copious and pleasant language, and in which a man can fully express his mind. It runs over a great tract of many countries, but it is not equally pure in all places.

Architectural style may have little to do with the main theme of *Utopia*, yet even here we find Prescott and More in agreement. Says Prescott:

The Peruvian architecture, bearing also the general characteristics of an imperfect state of refinement, had still its peculiar character; and so uniform was that character that the edifices throughout the country seem to have been all cast in the same mould.[15]

Means comments on the city of Cuzco:

The ancient streets ... are narrow and, on the whole, tolerably straight. Because of the massive, dark-hued masonry unrelieved by windows and having only a few doorways, the streets have a grim aspect ... [With] the immense stretches of unbroken wall the streets must have been drafty and chilly ... but impressive nevertheless.[16]

More comments in *Utopia:*

He that knows one of their towns, knows them all, they are so like one another, except where the situation makes some difference.

Their buildings are good, and are so uniform, that a whole side of a street looks like one house.[17]

To consider a very different phase of life, we find that both Peru and Utopia had a limited degree of religious freedom, with worship of Sun, Moon, and Stars, and of lesser gods, but also recognition of one supreme deity. Even some very unusual features are alike. For instance, according to Prescott:

The body of the deceased Inca was skilfully embalmed, and removed to the great temple of the Sun at Cuzco. . . .

They cherished a still stranger illusion in the attentions which they continued to pay to these insensible remains, as if they were instinct with life. . . . On certain festivals, the revered bodies of . the sovereigns were brought out with great ceremony . . . and entertainments were provided in the names of their masters . . . the guests partook of the melancholy cheer in the presence of the royal phantom with the same attention to the forms of courtly etiquette as if the living monarch had presided! [18]

The account in *Utopia* includes the following:

They believe it inconsistent with the happiness of departed souls not to be at liberty to be where they will, and do not imagine them capable of the ingratitude of not desiring to see those friends with whom they lived on earth in the strictest bonds of love and kindness; besides they are persuaded that good men after death have these affections and all other good dispositions increased rather than diminished, and therefore conclude that they are still among the living, and observe all they say or do.[19]

There are similar comments concerning their temples. Prescott relates:

. . . the most renowned of the Peruvian temples . . . consisted of a principal building and several chapels and inferior edifices, covering a large extent of ground in the heart of the city . . . and was so finely executed that a Spaniard who saw it in its glory assures us he could call to mind only two edifices in Spain which, for their workmanship, were at all to be compared with it.[20]

Again More is more brief, but in agreement: "They have magnificent temples, that are not only nobly built, but extremely spacious . . ." [21]

The attitude of the Peruvian toward augurs and astrology was similar, though unusual at that time. According to Prescott: "The illusory study of astrology, so captivating to the unenlightened mind, engaged no share of his attention." [22]

More again is in agreement: "They despise and laugh at auguries, and the other vain and superstitious ways of divination, so much observed among other nations . . ." [23]

In addition to More's incorporation into his *Utopia* of unusual and unideal features similar to those found in Inca society, there is another kind of evidence which would harmonize with the view that in *Utopia* he was describing an actual social order, and was not merely projecting his own views. In describing elements of social organization which did not then exist in any known European or Asiatic country, Thomas More specifically stated that he did not approve of the laws and customs which he described. Why should he cumber his account with unromantic, matter-of-fact descriptions of an economic system which was a figment of his own brain, only to reject important elements of that system? More was not the kind of person to write for entertainment only.

There are three reasonable explanations of his course. One is that he actually favored the doctrines he stated, but did not dare to espouse them publicly for fear of disapproval or persecution. J. H. Lupton, in editing the Latin and the first English edition of *Utopia,* took this view. He held that More wrote as he did "as an easy means, if necessary, of disavowing the serious intent of the whole of the Platonic fiction," and that the fact of no English translation's being made for a generation "would be thought strange, if we did not consider the political circumstances of the time." [24]

Another explanation is that More was passing on information he received from a traveler, and that he told the whole story, including the part he approved and the part he disapproved. This viewpoint is emphasized by the fact that he described various sordid and unlovely aspects of utopian ways, which in almost every particular correspond to Peruvian customs and laws. One of Thomas More's admirers, William Edward Campbell, in his *More's Utopia and His Social Teaching* holds specifically that More repudiated the major doctrine he went to such length to describe. Quoting from *Utopia* a dialogue between More and the traveler Hythloday, Campbell writes:

[Hythloday] having once again reasserted his principal contention "that until private property is taken away there can be no equitable or just distribution of things... nor can the world be happily governed," he listens to what More has to say in reply.

The reply is one of direct disagreement. "On the contrary," says More, "it seems to me that men *cannot* live conveniently where all things are held in common."

And he continues, "How can there be sufficiency of goods, or anything, where every man will withdraw his hand from labour." [25]

If More were passing on the description of a traveler, of a system he had heard about but did not himself approve, then this explanation would seem to be reasonable.

A third explanation is that he was describing and then refuting Plato, who is mentioned. Yet the likeness to Peru is much greater than the likeness to *The Republic*.

Do not the likenesses of Peru and *Utopia*, in incidental matters which have nothing to do with an ideal society, strongly reinforce the probability that Peru was the chief source of More's account?

The history of ancient Peru, as recorded by Spanish conquerors and as carefully reconstructed by painstaking research during the past century, leaves no doubt that a moneyless, propertyless economy, without wages or buying or selling, is not utopian in the sense of being "contrary to human nature," and therefore impossible, for this economy actually did operate successfully throughout a great empire and for a longer period than our nation has existed, while under that economy a people of many millions achieved an astonishing degree of social security.

The Peruvian social system should not be pictured as faultless. How much of the arbitrary policy of the Incas was due to effort quickly to convert savage and possibly indolent tribes into an orderly and civilized nation; how much was due to the technical primitiveness already described; and how much to the possible fact that only in dictatorship could such a high degree of discipline be achieved—these remain open questions.

The Peruvian standard of living must not be judged by the present age of technology. Means quotes another student of Peru, Louis Baudin, as saying, "In Peru the needs of the populace were few, and the Incas had a genius for preventing them from growing." [26] The very simple life, for high and low, was good public policy where there was neither machine power, nor animal power beyond the llamas that would carry scarcely more than a man. Security for all through long periods was better than intermittent affluence and famine.

Clements R. Markham, long president of the Hakluyt Society, in the course of fifty years' study of Peru, during which time he explored the country, learned the Inca language, translated records, and searched the archives and libraries of Peru and of Europe for documents, at the beginning of this century was perhaps the foremost authority on the Incas. In summing up his life studies in *The Incas of Peru,* he wrote:

. . . it seems certain that, under the very peculiar condition of Peru when the Incas ruled, the dreams of Utopians and Socialists became realities for a time, being the single instance of such realisation in the world's history.

A proof of the general well-being of the people is the large and increasing population. The *andeneria* or steps of terraced cultivation extending up the sides of the mountains in all parts of Peru, and now abandoned, are silent witnesses of the former prosperity of the country. The people were nourished and well cared for, and they multiplied exceedingly. In the wildest and most inaccessible valleys, in the lofty *punas* surrounded by snowy heights, in the dense forests, and in the sand-girt valleys of the coast, the eye of the central power was ever upon them, and the never-failing brain, beneficent though inexorable, provided for all their wants, gathered in their tribute, and selected their children for the various occupations required by the State, according to their several aptitudes.

This was indeed socialism, such as dreamers in past ages have conceived, and impractical theorists now talk about. It existed once because the essential conditions were combined in a way which is never likely to occur again. These are an inexorable despotism, absolute exemption from outside interference of any kind, a very peculiar and remarkable people in an early stage of civilisation, and an extraordinary combination of skilful statesmanship.

It was destroyed by the Spanish conquest, and the world will never see its like again.[27]

This was written by a man of eighty, thoroughly committed to the prevailing European type of civilization. Along with an historian's rigorous accuracy in finding and recording the facts, did he not have a conservative Englishman's aversion to socialist government?

We have noted that the fundamental social structure of Peru seems to have been an ancient and widespread folkway which had existed among democratically organized tribes throughout South America, as though it had sprung from a single root, long before the tribes began to cohere into great nations. Vespucci and other writers mention similar social organizations among the Indians along the Atlantic coast. Gerard Dudok, the Dutch writer, in his *Thomas More and*

His Utopia holds that More got some of his ideas from Vespucci's meager account of native social customs. More described a far higher culture than Vespucci met, and almost every point mentioned by Vespucci and included in *Utopia* was true, often to a larger degree, of Peru. That structure had continued in the large-scale organizations of Quito and other independent near-by nations before their conquest by the Incas and the completion of the great Inca empire. It did not, therefore, depend solely on an "extraordinary combination of skilful statesmanship." As in many other human societies, the centralized and despotic form of government seems to have been a final phase of a cultural cycle, and not an original characteristic of the Peruvian type of social economy. Philip Ainsworth Means, who, building on the foundation of Prescott's and Markham's researches, made Peru his life work, concluded that in ancient Peru the officials closest to the people, which it would appear constituted the large majority of all the administrative officials of the empire, were chosen by the people they governed.

Under another form of government the descendants of ancient Peru have not shown themselves to be a "peculiar and remarkable people." The European type of society which displaced their own has never recovered the former level of economic or social well-being, and even with the support of modern technology the region sustains far less than the ancient population.

The relative merits of the social order of ancient Peru and the European type of society prevailing there today are suggested by William Vogt, Chief, Conservation Section, Pan American Union. In the *Saturday Evening Post* for May 12, 1945, he wrote:

> Peru once, under the benevolent dictatorship of the Incas, grew wheat on the flanks of the Andes. It developed a system of stone-faced terraces, some of which have lasted to the present day. But,

according to Doctor Bennett, such terracing would now cost about $18,000 an acre....

Ancient Peru fed more people than now live in the country; according to the historians, there was enough for everybody. This was true during hundreds of years and, as one compares ancient terraces with modern soil erosion, one cannot help thinking the ancient Indians had a better chance of survival than their descendants. In modern Peru—as in most of the world—there are many hungry people.[28]

Is not Markham's dictum, "the world will never see its like again," the closest approach a competent historian could make to the conservative, long-held position that it never could happen at all? The real question is not whether it ever can happen again, but rather, whether it is a desirable kind of society to work for, and if not, whether some of its features are worthy of reproduction.

As Emerson, with his everyday Yankee manner, made many Americans into devotees of oriental philosophy without their knowing it, so have not More and Bellamy interested the world in the substance of the unique culture of this strange people? How remarkable that the significance of ancient Peruvian society, under its own name, has not been generally realized by authorities on social organization!

Do not most of the other great human cultures trace back finally to a common root? The unending surges of population over Asia and about the Mediterranean have carried social forms and mechanical skills back and forth until, in the entire region from Japan to Portugal, there is little that is completely separate in its origin.

In South America, in contrast, there existed almost the only great civilization which developed in complete independence of Europe and Asia, a civilization which seems to have grown almost entirely on its own roots. Separated from the main body of mankind so long ago that a great culture had developed which knew no written language, nor the use of the wheel and axle, the social structure of these people was to Europeans something new under the sun.

As stated heretofore, inquiry into the possible relation between the organization of society in Peru on the one hand, and *Looking Backward* and *Utopia* on the other, came about through searching Bellamy's writings for all possible hints as to his sources. Once attention was drawn to the likenesses between Peru and *Utopia*, they seemed too obvious to have remained unobserved for four hundred years. A search of the literature disclosed that H. Stanley Jevons had drawn attention to these parallels in a short article in the *London Times Literary Supplement* for November 2, 1935. As I did not see that article until after the foregoing chapter was written, the two suggestions are entirely independent in their origins. Jevons states that so far as he can learn, the similarities had not previously been observed.

He directs attention to "Ideas in *Utopia* which could not have been suggested by the experience of any country other than the Peru of the Incas and were unknown to fiction in More's time." Jevons draws attention to similarities, to some of which I had not alluded. Others I had already described. He says, "The most striking example connecting *Utopia* with the empire of Peru is the ornamentation of the priests' vestments with coloured feathers. . . . The description in *Utopia* is:

" 'The priests wear vestments of various colours of wonderful design, but not as costly material as one would expect; for they are not interwoven with gold or set with precious stones, but wrought with the different feathers of birds so cleverly and skillfully that no costly material could have equalled the value of the design. Moreover, in these birds' wings and feathers, and the fixed orders by which they are distinguished in the priest's vestment, they say certain hidden mysteries are contained.' "

Jevons continues: "This is almost a description of the elaborate cloaks worn by Incas of the royal family and high officials on state occasions. Several are preserved in museums, and they are almost covered with birds' feathers of various bright colours in striking and varied patterns. ... the clan and rank of the wearer were indicated in the pattern of the featherwork head dress and possibly also in the cloak. [Approximately the same was true of the Hawaiians, and the pre-Columbian natives of America from the Pueblo Indians of Arizona and New Mexico, and the Tarascans and Aztecs of Mexico, to the Mayans of Yucatan.] "

J. H. Lupton comments on the feather robes, "More's selection of this fanciful apparel for his priests may have been in pure whim, or in the endeavour to find something totally different from existing customs."

He comments also on the fact that in Utopia as in Peru other metals were in use, but that the production of iron was unknown. He mentions the public slaves in Utopia, mainly convicts, which compare with a similar class in Peru. He does not mention that the men serving the Inca's temples were descendants of rebels condemned to death, whose sentence was remitted on request of the Inca's wife.

Jevons comes to the following conclusion: "[More] being a lawyer ... would hesitate to repeat an extraordinary traveller's tale which he could in no way verify," and would be less subject to criticism by treating it as a fantasy. That More hesitated to associate his reputation with so strange a tale is indicated by the fact elsewhere noted, that he had it published in a foreign country, and in the text indicated his disagreement with major elements of the social order described. The names "Utopia" (nowhere) and "Hythloday" (wise in trifling matters) carried out this pattern of self-protection.

IV

Hythloday, First Circumnavigator?

THOMAS MORE DESCRIBES HYTHLODAY'S
return in the following words: "After he, with five
Castilians, had traveled over many countries, at last, by
strange good fortune, he got to Ceylon, and from thence to
Calicut, where he very happily found some Portuguese ships,
and beyond all men's expectations, returned to his native
country."

Several explanations of this passage are possible. It has
generally been taken as pure fantasy on More's part—he
was simply making a plausible story. It has been suggested
that More still thought South America to be part of Asia,
and that therefore his hero could easily reach India. This
latter supposition imputes to More an improbable ignorance
of current affairs, for by the time he wrote *Utopia* it was
generally known that America was a new world, and not a
part of the Asiatic continent.

So far as getting back to Spain or Portugal was concerned,
there was a well traveled trade route from the Inca Empire
north to the Caribbean Sea, at the mouth of the Magdalena
River, where Spanish vessels already were not infrequent.

Utopia was published three years before Magellan started
on his memorable voyage around the earth, but not until
after several Portuguese voyages had been made to India

and back around the Cape of Good Hope. On such voyages it was the almost uniform custom to sail westward from near the Cape Verde Islands to, or near to, Brazil, to take advantage of wind and currents, and then to turn southeasterly to round Africa. Hythloday might have retraced his course from Peru to the Atlantic coast, and there might have caught a Portuguese boat bound for India.

But there is still another possibility. Hythloday might have crossed the Pacific on the balsa craft of the Incas. The ancient Peruvians were not entirely a land-locked people. They constructed large sea-going rafts—balsas—made of seven to eleven or more water-resistant balsawood logs, which are lighter than cork, the larger logs in the center, giving the raft the shape of a pointed ship. They had keels and rudders, and were driven by oars and by canvas sails. One of them would hold fifty men, their supplies, and their llamas. Such an ocean-going craft, laden with a rich cargo, was met on the Pacific high seas by early Spanish explorers.*

At the time of the conquest of Peru by the Spaniards there

* As on other points, the writer found great differences of opinion concerning the seagoing quality of balsa rafts. Kenneth P. Emory, of the Bishop Museum in Honolulu, wrote definitely, "Balsa rafts become waterlogged in a few days if not taken out of the water to dry." Later he wrote that he received this information from the late Roland B. Dixon, and added, "Dixon was so emphatic about it being true that he caused me to modify my opinion that Peruvians may have reached Easter Island bringing the sweet potato and the masonry technique of cutting jogs in stones to make them fit together." (Letters to the author, February 3, 1941, and February 22, 1944.)

The writer then sought information directly from men responsible for the production of balsa timber. William T. Cox, of the U. S. Foreign Economics Administration, on April 15, 1944, informed the author that he had charge of increasing the yield of balsa wood from 6,000,000 to 35,000,000 feet per year. He was given this task because of his previous familiarity with balsa wood. He said, "I have seen balsa logs in floating log booms that had been floating for at least ten years. After long periods in the water they were still as buoyant as pine logs.

were records of a remarkable trip by one of the Incas to rich islands in the far west, across the Pacific. According to Philip Ainsworth Means, two of the greatest historians of ancient Peru, Sarmiento and Cabello de Balboa, record such a trip.

According to Sarmiento's *History of the Incas*, one of the Incas, Tupac Yupanqui, reached the Pacific Ocean in extending his conquests, some time before Columbus' discoveries (the Inca died in 1482). These historians relate that while the Inca was at the city of Tumbez on the Pacific coast, some native merchants returned by sea from the west. They told of islands where there were many people and much gold. The merchants had traveled on the balsa rafts.

The Inca determined to visit these distant lands, and sailed west with an immense fleet of balsas and twenty thousand men. After being gone nine months or a year, he returned with many black-skinned prisoners, gold, a chair of brass, and the skin and jawbone of an animal like a horse—there were no such animals in Peru.

In small floating docks and otherwise they remained floating for a good many years."

Christopher Walker, Chief of the Import and Export Section of the Lumber Division of the War Production Board, also is familiar with balsa in Ecuador and elsewhere. He states that there are three types of balsa wood in Ecuador, the most striking differences being in buoyancy and waterlogging. All three types may be found in a single stand of the timber. The lightest type is most resistant to waterlogging. Workers and their families build shelters on the rafts of balsa being brought down river and live on them for six weeks or more. When logs are left in floating booms, for the first year about three quarters of the log is out of water. After a year about half the log is out of water, and thereafter the buoyancy decreases very slightly. He thought it remarkable that such light porous wood should retain its buoyancy for so long. It is not treated in any way.

Thus, the experts' opinion that ancient Peruvians could not have traveled to the western islands because "balsa craft become waterlogged in a few days if not taken out of the water to dry" does not seem to be well founded.

The trophies were preserved in the fortress at Cuzco until the Spaniards came. The historian Sarmiento adds: "An Inca now living had charge of this skin and jawbone of a horse. He gave this account, and the rest who were present corroborated it." Sarmiento was so impressed by the account and by the trophies that he decided to seek those islands. He set out on an expedition and reached the Galapagos. Various writers have assumed that these were the islands mentioned by Sarmiento and Balboa. However, since the Galapagos Islands had neither human population nor gold, copper, or horses, they doubtless were not the ones reached by the Inca. In William Beebe's book, *Galapagos*, we find the statement: "They are one of the few places on earth where aboriginal man never existed"; and again, "Another feature of the islands is their complete uninhabitableness."

The next islands to the west are the Marquesas, about four thousand miles from Peru. The route from these to the East Indies was fairly well known to the South Sea Islanders. Though it may seem incredible that the Inca could have sailed that far, several bits of information seem to indicate such a possibility. On the Marquesas Islands are remains of great masonry structures, the origin of which is unknown to the present inhabitants.[1] Some of the individual stones weigh from three to ten tons. Concerning them Linton comments: "It is rather surprising to find the structural use of cut stone highly developed among a people otherwise as primitive as the Marquesans. Cut stone was more extensively used in the Marquesas than in any other part of Polynesia for which there are records." Since the Peruvians were past-masters of the art of cutting and transporting massive stone, the possibility that they visited and perhaps colonized the Marquesas Islands supplies one simple explanation.

One of the best pictures we have of the Marquesas Islands as they were before being overrun by white men is in Herman Melville's book *Typee*. In numerous particulars his account is suggestive both of Peru and of Utopia. He also tells of finding, in 1842, the vestiges of a past civilization, great stone terraces, three hundred feet long by sixty feet wide, built of stones ten to fifteen feet long and five feet thick. He wrote that the dwellings of the Islanders were almost invariably built on massive stone foundations. All over the islands there were other and more massive stone foundations. All these were of great age, and the natives had only vague legends concerning their origin.

According to Melville, religious rites and festivals in the Marquesas, though reflecting an elaborate development, seemed hollow and meaningless, as though they were the empty forms of an earlier culture. He relates that effigies of dead chiefs were kept in the company of the living. This might be an adaptation, in the moist climate of the Marquesas, of the Peruvian custom of similarly treating the mummies of their dead rulers as described in the quotation from Prescott in Chapter III.

The social economy of the Marquesas was very similar to that of ancient Peru. The land was held in common; the catch of fish was equally distributed to the whole population; the community united in building houses for individuals. As in Peru, there were no lawyers, no mortgages, no money. In Peru, in Utopia, and in the Marquesas, the women were exempted from heavy toil, and worked in wool and tappa or cotton. Both in Utopia and in the Marquesas we find a high regard for bodily health and beauty. In Peru, in Utopia, and in the Marquesas, the sick and disabled were fed along with the producers. The habit of reciting their history together in groups was common to all three.

The Marquesas Islands had the sweet potato, a native of America, which, very significantly, had there the same name it bore in Peru. Roland B. Dixon, after a very careful study, was convinced that the introduction of this plant into the

Marquesas and other islands preceded the coming of the Spaniards.[2] Like the Peruvians, the Marquesas Islanders used the "quipu," or strand of knotted cords, for keeping records, though their use of it was much simpler than in Peru.*

* The use of knotted cords for record keeping was not limited to Peru and to the Marquesas, but was almost world-wide. "A Pelew Islander, visiting England, knotted strings as a diary of all that struck him during his visit." (*Encyclopaedia Britannica,* Eleventh Edition, XXII, 762.) "In the Hawaiian Islands native carriers have knotted string records of their rounds." (*Ibid.*) The wampum of the North American Indians was more highly developed. Major Rogers in his *Account of North America* (London, 1765), wrote of its use: "The belts that pass from one nation to another in all treaties, declarations and important transactions are very carefully preserved in the chiefs' cabins, and serve not only as a kind of record or history but as a public treasury.... These strands and belts (of wampum) were the only visible records of the Iroquois, but they required the trained interpreters who could draw from their strings and figures the acts and intentions, locked up in their remembrance."—*Encyclopaedia Britannica,* Eleventh Edition, XXVIII, 320.

In the sixth century B.C. Lâo Tse, the Chinese philosopher, included in his teaching, "Induce people to return to [the old custom of] knotted cords, and to use them [in the place of writing]."—Chapter 80 of the *Tao-Teh-King* of Lâo Tse (translated by Dr. Paul Carus, Open Court Publishing Co., Chicago, 1898), p. 137. In commenting on this passage, Carus states that, "It is mentioned in Herodotus that the Persian King handed a thong with sixty knots to be used as a calendar for two months, to the Ionians whom he appointed guardians of a bridge over the Danube."

We see, therefore, that the use of knotted cords can be no sure indication of intercourse between Peru and lands to the west, though it strongly suggests that possibility. If there had been contact between Peru and Asia, it would seem that it occurred after the art of knotted cords developed, but before the art of writing (or the wheel and axle or the arch in architecture) had reached the eastern coast of Asia. Any later contact must have been casual or relatively recent, such as that of the Tumbez merchants or of the Inca Tupec Yupanqui.

Another suggestion occurs to the writer in considering this primitive

While pioneer travel from the East Indies eastward across the South Seas was by canoe, on some of the Pacific islands south of the Marquesas travel was by ocean-going rafts similar to those used in ancient Peru. Tradition has it that in old days some of these rafts were large enough to carry a thousand persons.

But it is not only in the Marquesas Islands that we have suggestions of Peruvian movements to the west.

While this chapter was in preparation the writer corresponded with Mr. R. Neil Williams, an amateur anthropologist of Bandoeng, Java. Mr. Williams is convinced that some East Indian cultures, as of the Toradjas of Celebes, bear evidence of ancient Peruvian origin or influence. He states: "The Toradjas are ancient émigrés from Peru, with textiles and dyeing materials known only to the Incas." He mentions identical tapestry work, mummy culture, artificial fertilizer, and terraced, irrigated agriculture. Since the massive architecture of Peru lacks any element of the arch, while closely comparable structures in the East Indies have a rudimentary keystone, he suggests that the drift of culture was westward from Peru. The westward equatorial currents, he asserts, would increase this probability. He writes, "There is so much evidence of the diffusion of American culture along the equator to the west that it is difficult to say

---

form of keeping records by knotted cords or by tally sticks. It was an excellent method of keeping quantitative records, that is, of numbers, but a poor method of recording qualitative ideas and emotions. The Peruvians had remarkable statistical records, but little philosophy. Is it not possible that in India and China as writing developed, the use of knots was no longer valuable for transmitting qualitative ideas, but was retained for numbers? Its form may have changed from knotted cords to the abacus. Perhaps here was the beginning of the separation of the two forms of language which play such distinct parts in modern life—the written language of qualitative thinking (literature) and the symbol language of quantitative thinking (mathematics).

which particular part it came from." Like the Incas of ancient Peru, the primitive Toradjas, he states, "have no idea of value, other than the value of use." He quotes "Dr. Van Dalen, who is head of the church at Depok," as stating that "the weaving, method of production, and dyeing was exactly like that practiced in Peru."

In a later letter Mr. Williams writes that the mummy wrappings of the Incas are identical in type with ceremonial headdress of the Toradja nobility, used also as burial cloths. He refers to an article by J. W. van Nouhuys in No. 4 of the tenth year of the periodical *Nederlandsch Indisch oud en Nieuw*. This view was supported, according to Williams, by Dr. Van Dalen, who "was a missionary in Galumpang in the upper Karama Territory in one of the least known Toradja districts. He collected a large number of these death cloths for the Colonial Museum . . . If this culture landed in Celebes it is quite natural for it to be found in other islands of the East Indies."

Mr. Williams included with his letter photographs of two "death cloths." One is a photograph of a Peruvian mummy wrapped in a death cloth, now in the British Museum; the other is of a Toradja death cloth from the Islands of Celebes. At last report it was in the Imperial Dutch Museum. The designs of these two death cloths are identical.

As every anthropologist knows, similarities of culture in different parts of the world are very numerous, and no single case, or even several cases, proves identity of origin. However, the repetition of such similarities is cumulative evidence. Those mentioned were picked up by the writer almost at random, without thorough search. If careful search and comparison should disclose many more cases of likeness, the results might be convincing. Such a study would need to be made deliberately and critically, without preconceived conclusions, for few persons are so intimately acquainted with both the culture of ancient Peru and those of the Pacific islands and the East Indies as to be equipped beforehand to make a dependable judgment. The writer has observed in his own profession that strong running currents of professional opinion may be traditional rather than critical in origin, and so he ventures to drop a suggestion in the hope of stimulating an unconventional approach to the question.

Had the traveler Hythloday reached Ceylon and Calicut from Peru, perhaps by way of the Marquesas Islands, he would have found the Portuguese already active in the East Indies, and might thus have found his way back to Europe. More states that Hythloday was a Portuguese, and had returned from the East Indies on a Portuguese vessel. In that case he might rank as the first man of historic record to circumnavigate the earth. The data presented are all too fragmentary to supply the basis for a conclusion, but may lead to an interest in the subject which will tend to throw more light on the possibility.

The idea of circumnavigation of the earth was not new with Columbus, Copernicus, Thomas More, or Magellan, or with the period which produced them. That idea of the rotundity of the earth, which, after being current among the Greeks for more than a thousand years, had been deliberately suppressed by the church in about the sixth century A.D., seems not to have been generally revived until *The Travels of Sir John Mandeville* was published in the late fourteenth century. In that miscellaneous collection of narratives, discourses, and legends which were compiled and presented over a century before Columbus' first voyage to America, there is lengthy discussion of how the pole star disappears as one travels south, while the Antarctic star appears and rises higher. The author states that from such observations other men have estimated the circumference of the earth to be 20,425 miles, whereas he calculates it to be 31,500 miles.[3] (The Greeks at Alexandria in about 200

B.C. had calculated the circumference of the earth as about 28,000 miles.)

The narrator in Mandeville's *Travels* insists that a man may go all around the earth, "as well under as above," and that "always he should find men, lands, and isles," and that those who dwell on one side of the earth "be straight feet against feet" of those who dwell on the other side. Then he continues with a story which might have supplied a suggestion to Thomas More, of "how a worthy man departed some-time from our countries for to go search the world. And so he passed Ind and the isles beyond Ind, where be more than 5,000 isles. And so long he went by sea and land, and so environed the world by many seasons, that he found an isle where he heard speak his own language. . . . whereof he had great marvel, for he knew not how it might be. But I say, that he had gone so long by land and by sea, that he had environed all the earth . . ." [4]

It has been said that no book was so generally read at the close of the fourteenth century as Sir John Mandeville's *Travels*.[5] Thomas More, therefore, would not have needed a traveler such as Hythloday to give him the idea of the circumnavigation of the earth.

Having presented the evidence conveniently at hand, both for and against the probability that More was describing an actual trip around the earth, we leave the question to those who may be intrigued by it.

PART TWO
THE UTOPIAN TRADITION

V

The Origins of Utopia

THE UTOPIAN TRADITION PROBABLY HAD many beginnings. Plato's *Republic,* believed to have been written between 390 and 370 B.C., often has been referred to as the original. Yet this is far from being the case. According to Aristotle, in his *Politics,* it was not Plato, but one Phaleas of Chalcedon, who "was the first to affirm that the citizens of a state ought to have equal possessions." Utopian writing had, in fact, become so common in Greece that, possibly even before Plato's *Republic* appeared, Aristophanes presented a burlesque of utopias—*The Ecclesiazusae,* or *Women in Parliament,* the more grotesque parts of which were aimed at proposals for relations of the sexes similar to those which were presented in the *Republic* and the *Laws.* The remainder of the theme, however, deals with the age-old problem of the economic organization of society. Had the following extract from this amusing travesty been published in 1888, just after Bellamy's *Looking Backward,* undoubtedly it would have been taken as a caricature of that work, and a point-by-point parallel could have been made of every item of utopian theory which it presents. In fact, Bellamy was accused of plagiarizing Aristophanes.

The plot of the comedy is that the women of Athens, disguised as men, appear in the parliament or assembly and vote that thereafter the women shall rule the city. In the following passages, Prexagora, the woman who was chief instigator of the plot and is now head of the women's government, outlines the new social order to her husband, Blepyrus, and to their neighbor, Chremes:

PREXAGORA: I've an excellent scheme, if you will but believe it;
But I cannot be sure how our friends will receive it;
Or what they will do, if the old I eschew,
And propound them a system erratic and new.
This makes me a trifle alarmed and faint-hearted.

BLEPYRUS: As to that, you may safely be fearless and bold;
We adore what is new, and abhor what is old.
This rule we retain when all else has departed.

PREXAGORA: Then all to the speaker in silence attend
And don't interrupt till I come to the end,
And weigh and perpend, till you quite comprehend,
The drift and intent of the scheme I present.
The rule which I dare to enact and declare
Is that all shall be equal, and equally share
All wealth and enjoyments, nor longer endure
That one should be rich, and another be poor,
That one should have acres, far-stretching and wide,
And another not even enough to provide
Himself with a grave: that this at his call
Should have hundreds of servants, and that none
at all.
All this I intend to correct and amend:
Now all of all blessings shall freely partake
One life and one system for all men I make.

BLEPYRUS: And how will you manage it?

PREXAGORA: First, I'll provide
That the silver, and land, and whatever beside
Each man shall possess, shall be common and free,
One fund for the public; then out of it we
Will feed and maintain you, like housekeepers true,
Dispensing, and sparing, and caring for you.

BLEPYRUS: With regard to the land, I can quite understand,
But how, if a man have his money in hand,
Not farms, which you see, and he cannot withhold,
But talents of silver and Darics of gold?

PREXAGORA: All this to the stores he must bring.

BLEPYRUS: But suppose
He choose to retain it, and nobody knows:
Rank perjury doubtless; but what if it be?
'Twas by that he acquired it at first.

PREXAGORA: I agree
But now 'twill be useless; he'll need it no more.

BLEPYRUS: How mean you?

PREXAGORA: All pressure from want will be o'er.
Now each will have all that a man can desire,
Cakes, barley-loaves, chestnuts, abundant attire,
Wine, garlands and fish: then why should he wish
The wealth he has gotten by fraud to retain?
If you know any reason, I hope you'll explain.

BLEPYRUS: 'Tis those that have most of these goods, I believe,
That are always the worst and the keenest to
thieve.*

* This criticism is identical with that made by Aristotle in his *Politics*
when discussing the utopias of the time.

PREXAGORA: I grant you, my friend, in the days that are past,
In your old-fashioned system, abolished at last:
But what he's to gain, though his wealth he retain,
When all things are common, I'd have you explain.

    .   .   .   .   .   .

BLEPYRUS: Just one other thing. If an action they bring,
What funds will be mine for discharging the fine?
You won't pay it out of the stores, I opine.

PREXAGORA: A fine to be paid when an action they bring!
Why bless you, our people won't know such a thing
As an action.

BLEPYRUS: No actions! I feel a misgiving.
Pray what are "our people" to do for a living?

CHREMES: You are right: there are many will rue it.

PREXAGORA: No doubt.
But what can one then bring an action about?

BLEPYRUS: There are reasons in plenty; I'll just mention one.
If a debtor won't pay you, pray what's to be done?

PREXAGORA: If a debtor won't pay! Nay, but tell me, my friend,
How the creditor came by the money to lend?
All money, I thought, to the stores had been
    brought.
I've got a suspicion, I say it with grief,
Your creditor's surely a bit of a thief.

CHREMES: Now that is an answer acute and befitting.

BLEPYRUS: But what if a man should be fined for committing
Some common assault, when elated with wine;

Pray what are his means for discharging that fine?
I have posed you, I think.

PREXAGORA: Why, his victuals and drink
Will be stopped by command for awhile; and I.
    guess
That he will not again in a hurry transgress,
When he pays with his stomach.

BLEPYRUS: Will thieves be unknown?

PREXAGORA: Why, how should they steal what is partly their
    own?

BLEPYRUS: No chance then to meet at night in the street
Some highwayman coming our cloaks to abstract?

PREXAGORA: No, not if you're sleeping at home; nor, in fact,
Though you choose to go out. That trade, why
    pursue it?
There's plenty for all: but suppose him to do it,
Don't fight and resist him; what need of a pother?
You can go to the stores, and they'll give you an-
    other.

BLEPYRUS: Shall we gambling forsake?

PREXAGORA: Why, what could you stake?

BLEPYRUS: But what is the style of our living to be?

PREXAGORA: One common to all, independent and free,
All bars and partitions for ever undone,
All private establishments fused into one.

BLEPYRUS: Then where, may I ask, will our dinners be laid?

PREXAGORA: Each court and arcade of the law shall be made
            A banqueting-hall for the citizens.

BLEPYRUS: Right.

. . . .

PREXAGORA: ... There'll be plenty for all, and to spare.
            No stint and no grudging our system will know,
            But each will away from the revelry go,
            Elated and grand, with a torch in his hand,
            And a garland of flowers in his hair.[1]

These early utopians, whom Aristophanes satirized here, and several of whom wrote during Plato's lifetime, did not begin the tradition. Three or four hundred years earlier, probably during the eighth or ninth century B.C., Lycurgus, according to tradition, was defining for Sparta a remarkable government and social order which he so carefully designed and so firmly established that it persisted for several centuries, and made Sparta the master of Greece. The Greek biographer, Plutarch, wrote, " . . . all those who have written well on politics, as Plato, Diogenes, and Zeno, have taken Lycurgus as their model, leaving behind them, however, mere projects and words; whereas Lycurgus was the author, not in writing but in reality, of a government which none else could so much as copy. . . ."

Plutarch, writing after about nine hundred years, seems to have the impression that Lycurgus created his system of government *de novo*. It is far more probable that the great Spartan lawgiver did not so much create a new order of society as regularize and codify the folkways of the people, bringing into the form of orderly law what before was only custom and tradition, perhaps with many crudities and incongruities. Otherwise acceptance of his code would have been less complete, for the intimate ways of the people are not quickly changed.

Probably about the time Lycurgus was establishing his regime at Sparta the Greek poet Hesiod, according to tradition, was singing utopian songs of the Hyperboreans. And then it is recorded that contemporaneously, or perhaps a century or two before, Homer sang of the Hyperboreans and the Aethiopians, at the opposite ends of the earth, each with utopian attributes. Probably Hesiod and Homer did not invent the themes of their songs. They doubtless were near the last of a long line of tribal bards who for ages had transmitted mythology, history, and folk songs by word of mouth, until some of their tales were captured and made more nearly permanent by the art of writing. Similarly, Plato's description of Atlantis doubtless reflects folk tales, common all the way from Arabia to Ireland, of a mystical land in the West where a good society prevailed.

But the Greeks were not alone among Mediterranean peoples in this building of utopias. A little way to the east, among the hills of Palestine, there was a parallel tradition.

Probably centuries before the themes of Homer had been reduced to writing, before Hesiod sang, or Lycurgus had given his laws to Sparta, the voice of the prophet Samuel had been raised in Palestine. Then, as time passed, the cities became corrupt, and the voice seemed to have died. But in herdsmen's cottages and on mountain pastures it was remembered. There developed or persisted in these communities a strong feeling against the evils of the times, and a dream of a better time to come.

This prophetic tradition evidently grew from generation to generation. Then among the rural people there appeared men of unusual power: Amos, about 760 B.C., and Hosea about twenty-five years later, are the first after Samuel whose names we know, who felt that they had a message from God. As with utopias of all ages, their messages begin with a denunciation of present evils, and proceed to a picture of a better day. Listen to Amos:

> ... I was no prophet, neither was I a prophet's son: but I was an herdman, and a gatherer of sycamore fruit: And the Lord took me as I followed the flock, and the Lord said unto me, Go, prophesy unto my people Israel.[2]

> Hear this, O ye that swallow up the needy, even to make the poor of the land to fail, Saying, When will the new moon be gone, that we may sell corn? and the sabbath, that we may set forth wheat, making the measure small, and the money great, and falsifying the balances by deceit? That we may buy the poor for silver, and the needy for a pair of shoes; yea, and sell the refuse of the wheat? ... Shall not the land tremble for this, and every one mourn that dwelleth therein? ... I will turn your feasts into mourning... I will make it as the mourning of an only son, and the end thereof as a bitter day ...[3]

> Though they dig into hell, thence shall mine hand take them; though they climb up to heaven, thence will I bring them down.[4]

He calls on the people to change their ways:

> Seek good, and not evil, that ye may live ... let judgment run down as waters, and righteousness as a mighty stream.[5]

But after such outbursts as these, the message attributed to the herdsman ends with a different tone, as it tells of the day when right living will have borne its perfect fruit:

> Behold the days come, saith the Lord, that ... the mountains shall drop sweet wine, and all the hills shall melt ... they shall build the waste cities, and inhabit them; and they shall plant vineyards, and drink the wine thereof; they shall also make gardens, and eat the fruit of them. And I will plant them upon their land, and they shall no more be pulled up out of their land which I have given them, saith the Lord thy God.[6]

A few years later condemnation of present evil and pictures of Utopia became more definite. What was begun by rude herdsmen was taken up by men of great emotional and literary power. The early temper of stern rigor grew into tenderness and compassion. The utopian message reached a high pitch with Isaiah:

... and they shall beat their swords into plowshares, and their spears into pruning-hooks; nation shall not lift up sword against nation, neither shall they learn war any more.[7]

And they shall build houses and inhabit them; and they shall plant vineyards, and eat the fruit of them. They shall not build, and another inhabit; they shall not plant, and another eat... They shall not hurt nor destroy in all my holy mountain, saith the Lord.[8]

Jeremiah and Ezekiel and others of lesser power further swelled the volume of these protests, and of the utopian dream. During this period there appeared another utopia, in the literary form of a message from Moses, though doubtless written centuries after his death, outlining a legal and social code and translating the general aspirations of the prophets into detailed application. Among advanced social ideas in this code were provisions that once every seven years all debts were to be cancelled and that all slaves and servants of their own people were to be liberated and given a start in life. To a degree which is not fully known, this utopian code of Deuteronomy actually became the law of the people.

But again the years passed, and the utopia was not realized. Then came a great prophet, who summed up all of the Hebrew utopian message and carried it further, so that his picture of Utopia, "the Kingdom of God on earth," has been the guiding star of men's aspirations for nearly two millenniums, its central theme being "Whatsoever ye would that men should do to you, do ye even so to them," and

"Thy Kingdom come, thy will be done, in reality as it is in Utopia."

With the Hebrews as with the Greeks the utopian message seems to begin between history and legend. Since they wrote on papyrus or parchment, it is probable that many of their earliest writings have perished. Yet the trail of Utopia is not entirely lost. In Egypt and Mesopotamia, where use of clay tablets gave greater permanence to writing, and where civilizations came to maturity much earlier, we can pick it up again.

An instance of incipient utopianism is contained in a letter to the Assyrian King Ashurbanipal, written about the middle of the seventh century B.C., not far from the time when the Greek bard Hesiod was singing, and when Amos was picturing his utopia to villagers of Palestine. According to Thorkild Jacobsen, of the Oriental Institute of the University of Chicago, "The writer hopes that the new king is to institute a period of bliss, to fulfill the utopian ideal, and he sees clear signs of it already": [9]

Ashur the king of the gods proclaims the name of the king my lord for the dominion of the land of Assyria. Shamash and Adad, through their steadfast regard for the king my lord (and) his dominion of the lands, have established a gracious reign, orderly days, years of righteousness, abundant rains, copious inundations, and acceptable prices. The gods are graciously inclined. The fear of god is strong. The temples cause prosperity. The great gods of heaven and earth are favorably disposed to the king my lord. Old men dance, the youth sing, matrons and maidens are gay with laughter. The women are taken in marriage, they are embraced, they bring sons and daughters to birth. Reproduction is blest. To him whose sin condemned to death, the king my lord has restored newness of life. Those who have been imprisoned for many years, you are set free. Those who have been sick many days are recovered. The hungry are satisfied. The lean grow fat. The destitute are supplied with clothing.[10]

And we may follow back the utopian theme in the Euphrates valley for still another two thousand years beyond King Ashurbanipal. To quote Jacobsen further:

From very early times the Sumerians had a clear and definite conception of what human society should be like. Their picture of the ideal state stresses respect towards parents and older brothers and sisters within the family, fair dealings and uprightness in relations with others, and particularly the idea of social justice. As is only natural in view of the fact that the Sumerians had a highly autocratic conception of the state, the person who was responsible for the realization and upholding of this ideal was the ruler.

Our earliest evidence of the existence of this ideal dates back to shortly after 2650 B.C. when Urukagina, ruler of Lagash, states as his obligation to prevent the mighty from harming the weak and defenseless, especially orphans and windows. From then on this ideal is often reflected in royal inscriptions and other literature. I may quote as a detailed example that the ruler Ishme-Dagan prays that the sungod, god of righteousness, "may place in my mouth righteousness and truthfulness" and that he will "make it my lot" to "give in right fashion judgments and decisions to the people," to deal well with the upright man, to destroy the criminal, "to have respect shown father, mother, and elder sister," to see that "the weak is not delivered up to the mighty," that "the powerful is not allowed to do according to his desire," that freemen are not put in fetters, "to destroy criminality and violence and to cause righteousness to grow." This example dates from shortly before 2200 B.C. From the references in royal inscriptions it is clear that this Utopian ideal was wholly accepted by Mesopotamian rulers, at least as an ideal. It may—as other Utopias—have had practical effects in shaping actual policies.[11]

Before such a statement would be made as a declaration of national policy it must have had a long period of incubation in the national mind.

Across the way in Egypt also, the utopian or messianic theme was having its long course of development. Dr. John A. Wilson, Director of the Oriental Institute, has described that tradition:

> There was messianism in Egypt at a very early date. The documents make this simply a return from a time of anarchy and disorder to "the good old days" of peace and prosperity. At times when there was distress in Egypt certain social prophets looked forward to the return of good and just rulers who would re-establish order and content in the land.
>
> The ancient Egyptian did not have directly a concept of an Atlantis as a distant country in which things were well ordered and life was plentiful. He did, however, have certain concepts which contributed to the idea of an Atlantis. There is a fairy tale of a sailor who was shipwrecked on an eastern island where life was abundant and good. In line with this is the designation of eastern countries in general as "god's lands." From Somaliland, Arabia, the eastern desert, and Syria-Palestine, the great sun god came as the sun rises on the eastern horizon. There is a vague feeling that "god's land" has certain desirable qualities, certain ideal aspects which Egypt does not have and which may be invisible in the geographic districts which I have listed. That thought plays into the fairy tale of the shipwrecked sailor and the ideal island.[12]

Ancient utopian tradition was not limited to the Mediterranean region. In the Far East at some unknown time, perhaps contemporaneous with Plato or a century earlier, "Dialogues of the Buddha" began to be passed from generation to generation by word of mouth, much as were the Homeric stories, until they were put in writing in Ceylon shortly before the beginning of the Christian era. The following passage, from the translation of T. W. Rhys Davids and his wife, is about a pacifist king who will reign in the far future, when the span of human life will be vastly extended, and when the only diseases or physical weaknesses known will be appetite, non-assimilation, and old age:

Among such humans, at Ketumati the royal city, there will arise Sankha, a Wheel-turning king, righteous and ruling in righteousness, lord of the four quarters, conqueror, protector of his people, possessor of the seven precious things. His will be these seven precious things, to wit: the Wheel, the Elephant, the Horse, the Gem, the Woman, the Housefather, the Councillor. More than a thousand also will be his offspring, heroes, vigorous of frame, crushers of the hosts of the enemy. He will live in supremacy over this earth to its ocean bounds, having conquered it not by the scourge, not by the sword, but by righteousness.[18]

We might guess that at the time this "dialogue" was originated, the wheel was a new and wonderful invention.

In India the utopian view attributed to Buddha did not hold an enduring place, while the accounts of the Golden Age in Hindu sacred literature tended to be pure mythology, with but slight suggestion that such conditions can be achieved by human effort. The Buddhist picture was also carried to China, but there it met no better fate. China already had its own utopias, coming down from the distant past, and by the time Buddhism reached there, an ingrained habit had developed of looking backward rather than forward for the Good Life.

In very ancient China utopian writings formed an important part of the classic literature. One of these, of about the close of the sixth century B.C., is "The Grand Course" of Confucius, which is quoted in the following chapter on "The Golden Age." This occurs in the seventh book of the *Li Ki*.[14]

The third book of the *Li Ki* also is a well developed utopia, known as the "Wang-Chih," or "Institutes of the King." [15] It dates probably from the first or second century B.C. It goes into some detail as to distribution of land, education, conservation of natural resources, budget-making, taxation, selection of men for civil service, and administration of justice. In its general purpose it might be compared with the book of Deuteronomy in the Old Testament.

The other great Chinese utopia dating from before the Christian era is the *Chow Li,* which forms one of the major Confucianist classics. In the opinion of Dr. Hu Shih, recently Chinese Ambassador to the United States, who has made a long study of Chinese utopias, this interesting political utopia is the outgrowth of an earlier work entitled *Chou Kwan,* of the second century B.C. Just as Plato's *Republic* was not wholly original in creation, but was the outgrowth of utopian thinking and writing of many centuries preceding, so it is highly probable that the utopias of Lâo Tse, Confucius, and others of those early centuries, harked back to similar utopian thinking and writing of still earlier days. This is specifically the opinion of many students.

After the Chinese utopians who wrote before the Christian era, according to Dr. Hu Shih, "for nearly twenty centuries of unified empire life there was very little original and courageous social and political thinking, and consequently practically no utopian writing worthy of the name. Much of the unorthodox political thinking took the form of commentaries or amplifications of the *Chow Li* which had become one of the major classics." [16] Again, according to Dr. Hu Shih, probably the only example of utopian writing in medieval China is a short essay of a few hundred words, "Peach Blossom Village," written in the fifth century of the Christian era. It pictures a village in which a group of families had found shelter and livelihood for centuries, free from taxation, wars, or devastation, but it attempts no positive political or social speculation. Since numberless remote villages in China have retained their prehistoric type of social organization down to the present century, it would seem not impossible that such a "utopia" would be an actual record of a small community which in an isolated nook had escaped the impact of the feudal age.

Passing over two barren millenniums we come to the most elaborate utopia in Chinese literature, the *Ching Hua Yüan,* or "Flowers in the Mirror," by Li Ju-Cheu.[17] Written through a period of years and finished about 1825, it is a novel of a hundred chapters. It was written partly as a way to make the public familiar with a phonetic system which the author had invented. The significance in Chinese usage of the title may be inferred from the quotation, "perhaps for us that future will be as illusory as *flowers in the mirror,* or the reflection of the moon in the rippling stream." In comparison with the matter-of-fact *Utopia,* or "nowhere," of Thomas More, the lighter touch of this title is characteristically Chinese.

The setting of the story is in the reign of Empress Wu, about A.D. 700. One part of thirty-three chapters is an imaginary account, somewhat in the manner of *Gulliver's Travels,* of a visit of Tang Ao and his friends to distant countries and strange peoples. Some of these are grotesque stories, as of a country where men had such large ears that in sleeping they would use one for a mattress and the other for a cover. Others suggest modern inventions, such as flying carriages, illustrated as operated by propellers. Most of the chapters are intended to point out existing evils of Chinese society, and to picture better ways of living, as is the case with utopias the world over. A part of one of these sketches, "The Country of Great Men," is quoted in the chapter on "The Golden Age."

Another, "The Country of Gentlemen," is particularly utopian. In it men high and low, rich and poor, mutually respect each other's feelings without reference to the wealth

or social status of either; and this after all is the essence
of what constitutes a true gentleman. The name of the country would have a utopian inference to the Chinese mind, as
it was a cardinal teaching of Confucius that the world will
be civilized when it is inhabited by gentlemen.

Still another Chinese utopia, the *Ta T'ung Shu,* or "The
Great Unity," by K'and Ye-wei, though written in 1884, has
only recently been published. This has been reviewed by
Chi-Chen Wang. Taking for his text the Confucian utopia,
"The Grand Course," the author develops his theme meth-
odically. He holds that man is by nature kind, and that he
is inclined to seek happiness and avoid suffering. Because of
perversion of our nature by our institutions, suffering is the
chief reality of human life. He describes the sources of
sorrow and the causes of suffering, and proposes a program
for their gradual elimination by such means as world government, abolition of classes and mixing of races, improvement of diet, equality of the sexes, abolition of the family,
education, communal government, kindness to animals, and
labor-saving technology.

We see that, widespread as has been the urge to visualize
a good society, its development has been far from uniform.
Icelandic scholars report that little of the utopian theme
appears in Scandinavian literature until after the coming of
Christianity from the south.

The Scandinavian Edda, *Voluspo,* contains most of the
elements characteristic of utopias—strife, corruption, defeat,
and a picture of a better world. War comes to earth, and the
gods fight with the Wanes:

> On the host his spear did Othin hurl,
> Then in the world did war first come;
> The wall that girdled the gods was broken,
> And the field by the warlike Wanes was trodden.[18]

Evil times come to the earth, and after much stress and battle the earth is destroyed:

> Brothers shall fight and fell each other,
> And sisters' sons shall kinship stain;
> Hard is it on earth, with mighty whoredom;
> Axe-time, sword-time, shields are sundered,
> Wind-time, wolf-time, ere the world falls;
> Nor ever shall men each other spare.[19]

> . . . .

> The sun turns black, earth sinks in the sea,
> The hot stars down from heaven are whirled;
> Fierce grows the steam and the life-feeding flame,
> Till fire leaps high about heaven itself.[20]

Finally a new earth rises, and a good day comes:

> Now do I see the earth anew
> Rise all green from the waves again;
> The cataracts fall, and the eagle flies,
> And fish he catches beneath the cliffs.[21]

> . . . .

> In wondrous beauty once again
> Shall the golden tables stand mid the grass,
> Which the gods had owned in the days of old.[22]

> . . . .

> Then fields unsowed bear ripened fruit,
> All ills grow better, and Baldr comes back;
> Baldr and Hoth dwell in Hropt's battle-hall,
> And the mighty gods: would you know yet more? [23]

> More fair than the sun, a hall I see,
> Roofed with gold, on Gimle it stands;
> There shall the righteous rulers dwell,
> And happiness ever there shall they have.[24]

This poetic story, probably composed about a thousand years ago and reduced to writing a few centuries later, may have been indirectly influenced by the Christian tradition. It is perhaps the nearest to a utopia which has survived from early Norse literature.

Across the ocean, in the land of the Aztecs, there was a utopian tradition of great antiquity. J. H. Cornyn, the Aztec scholar, translator of the "Song of Quetzalcoatl," has given us a picture of "The Promised Land of the Nahuas":

The later Nahuatl races, to which the Toltecs and Nahuas belonged, had a well-defined tradition of a promised land where life would be ever pleasant and the soil ever fruitful. This promised land was both behind them and before them. Huemac, guider of the first exodus of Toltecs from their mythical home in the north, led his people, before the beginning of the Christian era, toward Temoanchan (*temoa*, they seek, *in*, their, *chan*, home; that is, the home they are seeking), where power, glory, and felicity awaited them. Temoanchan was compared, by the Nahua poets, to the home of the earth gods in the highest mountains. It was, therefore, a terrestrial paradise to which Huémac led his people.

Upwards of a thousand years later, other Toltecs, under another great leader, transformed the tradition of Huemac into that of Quetzalcoatl, messenger of the gods, who brought to them from the Sun the culture of the Sunland and instituted in the Valley of Mexico, the golden age to which, later on, Aztec poets looked back with unrestrained admiration and longing. For they believed that this vanished glorious age was to return with even greater splendour, power and glory for the Nahuatl people.

"The Song of Quetzalcoatl," the greatest of the sagas of the American Indian races, recounts the mythical struggle that took place between Quetzalcoatl, the Wind God, and Tezcatlipoca, the Moon God, in Tula, the famous Toltec capital, the highway to which was "traveled all the daytime, traveled all the night-time." Tezcatlipoca, with his arts of enchantment, brought un-numbered plagues upon Tula. Toward the end of the eleventh century, the famous city was destroyed and the Toltecs scattered to the four winds of heaven. The enemy forced Quetzalcoatl to leave the city and to return to the Sun from which he had come on his mission of culture. Leaving the coast of the Gulf of Mexico, Quetzalcoatl sent back four of his followers to govern Cholula, the later metropolis of the Toltecs, promising them that he would return and take from the hands of their descendants the government of Mexico; and that his regime would be more regal, happier and more glorious than that of the vanished golden age of the Toltecs.

According to this legend the land of Tula was rich beyond all comparison; there the corn-ears were so big one could scarcely embrace them with the outstretched arms, and the cotton grew in all shades and colors so that "no need was there to dye it." * There was untold wealth in Tula and no one was ever in want. This was the golden age to which the Aztecs looked back and of which their poets sang in rapturous verse. But it was also the paradise to which they looked forward with longing and anxiety, with the return of the Wind God, in all his majesty, power and glory.

*Compare with the utopian Fourth Eclogue of Virgil: "the ram shall of his own accord, even while at pasture, change the colour of his fleece, now into sweet-blushing purple, now into saffron hue. Scarlet shall spontaneously clothe the lambs as they feed." [Bryce, A. Hamilton, trans., *The Works of Virgil* (London, George Bell & Sons, 1907), p. 22]

In the science column of the *New York Times* for January 9, 1944, we read: "The day may be not far distant when a woman may choose the color of her dress from the plant as the result of work done by the Russians and the Delta Experimental Station of Mississippi. No dyes are used. The color is nature's own. . . . The Russians claim to have developed color-fast lints in red, green, auburn, dark brown, blue and khaki."

So unquestionably was this tradition believed by the Aztecs that Montezuma II, convinced that Cortes was the expected Quetzal-coatl come back to govern the land, dared not, famous warrior though he was, offer resistance to the Spaniards. The great tragedy of destruction of the Aztec empire was largely due to this native expectation of the coming of an age happier and more glorious than that of the gold days of the Aztecs.[25]

The lore of the North American Indian, so far as we have found, has little of that element, though among the Iroquois there were traces or beginnings of utopian expectation. It is interesting that the Aztec utopian god, Quetzal-coatl, is represented as a white man, and as having come from the East.

In Japan, as in medieval China, utopian writing has played a negligible part. Some modern Chinese utopias, such as *The United States of the World,* by K'ang Yeow Wei, seems certainly to be inspired from the West.

Man's conscious aspiration for a good life in the future, with deliberate effort to picture the conditions of a good society, found its fullest and perhaps its highest early expression near the eastern shores of the Mediterranean.

How far back of the ancient clay tablets of Assyria, of the writings of Lâo Tse and Confucius, of the traditions of Ceylon, and of the legends of the Aztecs, would it be necessary to go to reach the beginning of the utopian dream? We do not know. Every animal as it grows from infancy, every plant as it springs from a seed, seems to be moved by an inner impulse to fulfill the type through which it must find expression. The drive to realize an ideal is a universal, inherent characteristic of life itself. Since man cannot read the minds of other animals, he may claim to be the sole possessor of conscious design for his future, having a monopoly of visions of a good society in a good world. We might define man as the animal that makes utopias.

As we trace the growth of Greek and Hebrew utopian traditions, we are tempted to suggest that these two views of a future good society had a common origin in the distant past, perhaps the same origin as that of similar traditions in the valleys of the Nile and the Euphrates, and that, some time before the earliest recorded Greek literature, they became divided. Thereupon each may have developed according to the genius of the people, and each took its separate course for many more years. Let us pick up these utopian threads where we left them—the Greek tradition with Plato's *Republic,* and the Christian utopia with the "Sermon on the Mount"—and carry them forward.*

In Greek and Roman literature there are many utopian expressions, though many of them are dominantly mythological or idyllic, too far removed from reality to influence the actual course of events. Virgil's Fourth Eclogue, written about 40 B.C., which is typical of much of this writing, was made famous by efforts to interpret it as a forecast of the coming of Christ.

It was about A.D. 100 that the Greek, Plutarch, wrote his *Lycurgus,* the lawgiver of very ancient Sparta, who had lived about nine hundred years before. How much this is a true biography, and how much it is a utopia by Plutarch, authorities are not agreed. *Lycurgus* has had far-reaching influence as a chief inspiration for numerous later utopian writers.

Then, nearly three hundred years after Plutarch wrote *Lycurgus,* there appeared another picture of an ideal society, this time in the Hebrew-Christian tradition, St. Augustine's *City of God,* completed in A.D. 426. J. O. Hertzler, in his *History of Utopian Thought,*[26] says of this work, "It played an important part in the plans of kings and popes, and the schemes of empires and hierarchies." In his *City of God* Augustine showed that it was not the giving up of paganism

---

* Jesus, living in Greek-cultured Galilee, was influenced by Greek Stoicism as well as by Hebrew prophetical thought. They were united in him.

from which Rome was suffering, but rather a failure to live according to Christian principles. He pictured a universal order in which peace with God would be followed by peace among men, an order in which the church would be the dominant institution, with governments as its instruments.

As in China the utopian spirit, after an early vigorous growth, lay dormant for nearly two thousand years until it was quickened into fresh life by contact with new ideas and new patterns of living from other continents; so also in the western world it appears that the utopian impulse, so vigorous around the shores of the Mediterranean in an earlier age, was not strong enough of itself to stimulate a radically new vision in medieval Europe. There it required the greater stimulus of knowledge of a remarkable social order in a hitherto unknown land.

Unless we should class Dante's *De Monarchia* among utopias, we have an interval of nearly eleven hundred years between St. Augustine's *City of God* and the next great utopia with which the western world is generally familiar— More's *Utopia*. It should not be assumed that the utopian view was wholly absent during this long period. The same urge was latent in men's spirits and frequently flamed up.

For instance, there is that compilation of ancient and medieval lore and legend already referred to, known as *The Travels of Sir John Mandeville*. This miscellaneous collection which, even as a Mandeville compilation in the 1370's, dates from more than a century before Thomas More, contains a brief utopia, "Of the Goodness of the Folk of the Isle of Bragman." Of them the account states:

And, in general, all the men of those isles and of all the marches thereabout be more true than in any other countries thereabout, and more rightfull than others in all things. In that isle is no thief, ne murderer, ne common woman, ne poor beggar, ne never was man slain in that country ... And they prize none

earthly riches; and so they be all rightfull. And they live full
ordinately, and so soberly in meat and drink, that they live right
long. And the most part of them die without sickness, when nature
faileth them, for eld.[27]

According to this account, when Alexander the Great undertook to conquer them, they sent couriers to him with the
message:

What may be enough to that man to whom all the world is
insufficient? Thou shalt find nothing in us, that may cause thee
to war against us. For we have no riches, ne none we covet, and
all the goods of our country be in common. Our meat, that we
sustain withal our bodies, is our riches. And, instead of treasures
of gold and silver, we make our treasure of accord and peace, and
for to love every man other ... We have been in perpetual peace
till now, that thou come to disinherit us ... For justice ne hath
not among us no place, for we do to no man otherwise than we
desire that men do to us.[28]

Whereupon, the account states, Alexander left them alone.
Quintus Curtius, first century, in his life of Alexander,
includes a message presumably sent him by another people of
simple life, the Scythians:

If the gods had wished the disposition of your body to be equal
to the avidity of your mind, the world would not have held you.
... What is your business in this land of ours? We have never
touched the borders of yours. ... We can serve no man nor do we
desire to command any. That you may not be ignorant of the
Scythian people, know that we have our gifts, the yoke, the
plow, the spear, the arrow, the cup. We use these both with our
friends and against our enemies. We give to our friends the
grain grown with the labor of our oxen; we pour libations of wine
from the cup to these gods; we seek our distant enemies with the
arrows, those close at hand with the spear. ... Your wars are the

children of your victories. For although you may be greater and stronger than anyone else, yet no one wishes to suffer foreign dominion.

You will know that though their country stretches far and wide, you will none the less never capture the Scythians. Our poverty will be swifter than your army which carries the booty of so many peoples.... Those upon whom you will not wage war, you may always enjoy as good friends. For friendship is strongest among equals and they appear equal who have not made a test of their strength against each other.[29]

The story of the Isle of Bragman may have had a similar early origin.

In harmony with the general habit of utopians, the *Travels* included not only this picture of a good society, but descriptions of evil conditions in other lands, which in effect were shrewd criticisms of prevailing evils in Church and State in Europe.

Because More, when he published *Utopia* in 1516, about twenty-five years after the discovery of America, seemed to break the silence of a thousand years, he has commonly been looked upon as an original genius who, out of his own mind and experience, created a picture of an ideal society.

The fact is, however, as a brief view of his background will indicate, that few writers of utopias were less definitely original or more certainly the product of their times or their environments. In earlier chapters the debt of Thomas More to ancient Peru has been discussed. While much of *Utopia* is in effect an account of the social structure of the Inca state, that source did not by any means set the limit to his possible borrowing. The following account, mostly written before the Peruvian source was discovered by the author, indicates some of the other influences which may have acted upon More. It is evident that, while he followed the Inca pattern, More wove into it much of the thought and feeling of the Mediterranean utopian tradition and of the spirit of western Europe.

As already noted, when in 1485 the two young Oxford students, Linacre and Grocyn, visited Italy, they came home on fire with the new learning, and began the teaching of Greek at Oxford. Thomas More, then a boy of sixteen, was one of their pupils. The introduction into Oxford of Greek, including the pagan Plato, was a serious matter. The elder More, fearing that his son would be contaminated, took him out of Oxford, though not until friendships had been formed which lasted throughout his life.

By far the most important of these friends was John Colet, son of a London merchant, and twelve years older than More. In 1494 Colet went to Italy for two years. There and on his travels back and forth he seems to have come in contact with several powerful utopian currents. One was the re-emergence of the prefeudal, democratic, communal life of northern Europe, combined with simple Christianity, strikingly in contrast with the decadence and corruption of the church which then prevailed. According to Frederic Seebohm in his *Oxford Reformers,* Colet found this sincere devotion and high ethical quality in some primitive German monks with whom he stayed for a time, and probably also in the powerful personality and sermons of Savonarola, then at his best in Florence. At the Platonic Academy, Pico della Mirandola was becoming a devout disciple of Savonarola and, perhaps unconsciously, was striving for a harmony between the teachings of Plato and those of the founder of Christianity.

Colet returned to England a deeply convinced disciple both of the new Greek learning and of a regenerated and purified Christianity. A year or two later, Erasmus, the young Dutch student who was to go down in history as one of the great minds of his age, came to England on the first of his several visits. At Oxford and in London this little group of friends—Colet, Linacre, Grocyn, More and Erasmus—began their lifelong friendship and their life work. Colet's was the dominating mind and spirit. He largely guided the thinking and feeling of More and remade that of Erasmus, who said of him, "When I listen to my friend Colet it seems to me like listening to Plato himself." He was a man of very great, thoroughly trained, and widely informed intelligence, of fine ethical quality, of practical capacity, and of unusual fearlessness.

He summed up and endeavored to find unity in Plato and the Greek tradition, the Hebrew prophets and Jesus, St. Augustine and his *City of God*, Savonarola and his idealized state, the primitive Christianity which was emerging, or persisting, in Germany, and the practical life of an Englishman. He was one of the first of the modern world to have a truly scientific temper, in that he was committed to full and free inquiry. He had a conviction which is a characteristic of any real faith—that sincere, open-minded search for the truth will not lead men astray.

Seebohm, in his *Oxford Reformers*, writing of the *Novum Instrumentum* of Erasmus and the *Utopia* of More, comments that it is remarkable "that two such works, written by two such men, should, in measure, be traceable to the influence and express the views of a more obscure but greater man than they. Yet, in truth, much of the merit of both these works belongs indirectly to Colet." [30]

Through Colet and his group, as expressed by Thomas More in his *Utopia*, the two lines of utopian thought which in the Greek and Hebrew traditions had been too widely separated since the beginning of the Christian Era, were again united and were added to the democratic community tradition of Britain and northern Europe.

Utopia was the work of a man under forty, who became more conservative with the years. As the forces of reaction gradually overwhelmed John Colet's group, some moved toward Wyclif and a free, indigenous, English expression of religion, while others moved toward Rome. More was among the latter. In his later years he made life a burden for certain active Protestants.

Quite probably *Utopia* had in it something of the spirit of Colet, as well as of More's own genius. It breathes an English spirit which he later came to oppose—the spirit of Wyclif and of *Piers Plowman*. Wyclif, who lived a century and a half earlier than More, was perhaps the greatest religious mind that appeared in Europe for a thousand years. Huss directly and Luther indirectly were his spiritual children. His English version of the Bible and his traveling preachers, the Lollards, rooted the spirit of freedom and genuine piety so deeply in English life that reaction and oppression never killed it.

The great English poem, *Piers Plowman*, of the 1360's and 1370's, has in it so much of inspired common sense as to suggest that its origin was not unassociated with Wyclif's ideas. The headquarters of Wyclif were at Oxford, and although his movement was formally suppressed in the University, it probably continued there informally, as it did all over England. Even with the lack of specific documentary evidence, it seems most likely that Colet and his followers came into possession, not only of the tradition of Greece and Italy, but also of the spirit of Wyclif, the Lollards, and *Piers Plowman*, to which the English spirit is so largely indebted.

W. H. Fyfe, in an article entitled "Tacitus's Germania and More's Utopia," [31] draws attention to the very great similarity of some of the sentences of *Utopia*, which was written in Latin, to sentences in the *Germania* of Tacitus. The Latin style and use of words, he holds, are strikingly alike. Along with this similarity in form and tone are certain likenesses of description, such as the statement in each that women accompanied their husbands into battle, though that particular point might have been taken from Plato's *Republic.* The attitude toward suicide, and the habit of mothers of nursing their own children, are similar. Tacitus's *Germania* had been published in Venice in 1470 and may have been brought to England by More's friends, who spent some time in Venice.

Thus More's *Utopia*—though it seems suddenly to have appeared after a gap of more than a thousand years, during which almost the only ideal society men wrote about was in another world—was no new creation, without intellectual parentage. As clearly as any other utopian writing it has its roots in the past. At no earlier moment could one mind have united these great traditions: the classic Greek view of life; the essential ethical spirit of the Hebrew prophets and of Jesus, which expressed itself in revulsion against the injustice of the time; the democratic community spirit of England and northern Europe; and the new spirit of open-minded, critical, scientific inquiry, which, since the days of Greece and early Rome, had found little freedom of expression.

Just how much Thomas More borrowed from Herodotus, from Plato, from Plutarch's *Lycurgus,* from St. Augustine's *City of God,* and from Tacitus's *Germania,* has been the subject of much speculation. It is doubtful whether a great deal of additional light will ever be thrown on that question. When we come to measure the relative weight of the various traditions in the content of More's *Utopia,* we find that the new, strange tradition of ancient Peru seems to outweigh them all and substantially fixes the social pattern which More presents, but we also find that it is interwoven with many elements from other sources.

Almost exactly a century after More's *Utopia,* three other utopias appeared within a short time. Perhaps the first of these to be written, *The City of the Sun,* by Campanella, was last to be published, about 1623. This took its name, as well as part of its theme, from Peru. According to Felix Held, though it was published last of the three, it was written first and was read in manuscript by the German, Johann Valentin Andreae, whose utopia, *Christianopolis,* written in 1615, appeared in 1619. Again according to Held, Andreae's work largely determined the form and content of two other utopias, Bacon's unfinished *New Atlantis,* published posthumously, and Golt's *Nova Solyma,* published in 1648. Held states that Andreae's work was the original stimulus for the organization of the British Royal Society. At about the same time appeared Harrington's *Oceana,* 1656. In 1726 came Swift's *Gulliver's Travels.* R. W. Chambers, in his *Thomas More,* writes, "From some aspects Swift seems to be More come to life again." In *Gulliver* the author gives *Utopia* the honor, rare with him, of direct and repeated imitation, and he repays his debt by depicting Thomas More as the one modern man worthy to rank with the five noblest men of antiquity.

From that time to the present, except for a few periods of relative inactivity, there has been a steady flow of utopias in nearly all European languages. It has been estimated that perhaps a thousand have been published in English alone. With the possible exceptions of Campanella and of Morelly, who wrote *The Basiliade,* not until Edward Bellamy appeared did another utopian writer follow Thomas More in consciously using the new, great utopian tradition, which had its roots in a different culture from those about the Mediterranean.

VI

The Golden Age

THE ANCIENT FABLES OF THE GOLDEN AGE
were not all fabulous. Many of them had foundations
of fact. Some of them were more or less shadowy records
of societies which had excellent traits, appealing to the cravings of men for a good society. They gave reason for hope
and belief that the traits which ought to characterize society
are not impossible of achievement. What has been, may be
again. If this is a sound inference from the facts, then there
is no reason for withdrawing from men this reason for hope.

There were two general lines of Greek tradition concerning an ideal society. The expression "The Golden Age"
originally referred to a specific element in Greek mythology
which attempted to account for the origin of mankind. This
tradition was similar to far earlier mythologies of Mesopotamia and India, and probably all had a common origin.
They are almost purely mythological, and have little suggestion for the actual conduct of society.

Parallel with this mythology were legends of strange
peoples, either of an earlier age or dwelling in remote parts
of the world, who embodied ideal personal and social qualities. These range from almost pure mythology or fantasy
through all degrees of realism to what seem to be straight-
forward factual accounts by travelers, or factual accounts of

earlier states of local societies. As the centuries passed, there was a fusing of the mythological with the historic, until often no division line is evident. The expression "The Golden Age," like the Platonic word "ideal," has gradually been broadened and blurred in its meaning, until in common usage it has come to be applied to any legendary age in which excellent conditions prevailed. It is chiefly in the sense of possible, actual good societies in the past, rather than of purely mythological tradition, that the term is used here.

The oldest clear expression of the Golden Age mythology in Greek literature is in Hesiod's collection of myths and legends, *Works and Days*, probably of the eighth century B.C. Describing the five ages of the world, he begins with the Golden Age:

> First of all the deathless gods having homes on Olympus made a golden race of mortal men. These lived in the time of Cronus when he was king in Heaven. Like gods they lived with hearts free from sorrow and remote from toil and grief; nor was miserable age their lot, but always unwearied in feet and hands they made merry in feasting, beyond the reach of all evils. And when they died, it was as though they were given over to sleep. And all good things were theirs. For the fruitful earth spontaneously bore them abundant fruit without stint. And they lived in ease and peace upon their lands with many good things, rich in flocks and beloved of the blessed gods.[1]

With the disappearance of the men of the Golden Age the gods created in succession a race of silver, then a race of bronze, who destroyed themselves by their own hands, then a race of heroes, who also died in warfare, and finally a race of iron—our own. This story, with endless variations and interpretations, was worked over by Greek and Roman poets and philosophers for a thousand years. Half a century before Aristophanes wrote his parody on social utopias, various

Greek poets produced satires on the myth of the Golden
Age. Lovejoy and Boas reproduce or mention half a dozen
such. The following by Teleclides (about 440 B.C.) is typical:

I shall then recount from the beginning the life which I provided for mortals. First there was peace among all things like
water covering one's hands. And the earth bore neither fear nor
disease, but all needed things appeared of their own accord. For
every stream flowed with wine, and barley cakes fought with
wheat cakes to enter the mouths of men, pleading to be gulped
down if they loved the whitest. And fishes, coming to men's
houses and baking themselves, would serve themselves upon the
tables. And a river of soup flowed by the couches, swirling hot
meats. And pipes conducting sharp sauces ran beside those wishing
them, so that there was a plenty to moisten one's mouthfuls and
permit one to swallow them tender. And on the dishes would
appear honeyed barley cakes strewn over with spices, and roasted
thrushes with milk cakes flew down one's gullet. And there were
pancakes elbowing each other aside at one's jaw and shouting
their war cries.[2]

Kirby Flower Smith writes: "As the Golden Age ceased
to be an article of faith, it became, more and more, the field
in which these thinkers aired their theories of what the
world ought to be. From this sort of thing it was only a step
to that long line of Utopian romances which were quite as
characteristic of late antiquity as they are of the present day." [3]

Legends of supposedly actual good societies kept pace with
sheer mythology. Smith states:

Piety and justice as *motifs* in the ideal of happiness had been ascribed, long before Hesiod's time, to peoples living beyond the
limits of the known world. Such were Homer's *Abioi* (Il. xiii. 6),
"the most righteous of men," and, to give one more example, the
Hyperboreans, so long famous in the literature and legend of the
Graeco-Roman world.[4]

Not only remote peoples but distant times contributed to these legends. Sophisticated Rome, looking back to the simple democratic life of its beginnings, celebrated that idyllic memory at the Saturnalia, which still survives in diluted form in the New Year's celebrations of our larger cities. This description is by Pompeius Trogus (first century):

The first inhabitants of Italy were the Aborigines, whose king, Saturn, is said to have been so just that there were no slaves under him nor any private property, but all things belonged to all in common and undivided, as if all men had one patrimony. In memory of this precedent it was decreed that during the Saturnalia, by a leveling of all men's rights, slaves should sit down at banquets with their masters indiscriminately.[5]

Among the more purely mythological stories of distant peoples were those concerning the Hyperboreans of the far north and the Aethiopians of the south, though even in these accounts there are traces of reality. While the tradition is at least as old as Homer, a description by Pomponius Mela, of the first century, is typical:

On the Asiatic shore the Hyperboreans are first found, lying beyond the Northwind and beyond the Rhiphaean mountains and under the very pole. There the sun does not rise every day as among us, but having arisen first at the time of the vernal equinox, it does not sink until the autumnal. Thus there is a continuous day of six months and a night of another six. The narrow sunny land is spontaneously fertile. The inhabitants are very just and live longer than any other mortals and more happily. In fact, always happy with festive leisure, they know neither wars nor altercation. ... They inhabit woods and groves; and when sufficiency of living rather than boredom has come upon them, laughingly they wreath their heads with garlands and throw themselves headlong into the sea from a certain rock. This is their strange funeral rite.[6]

Most conspicuous among actual historic peoples to whom utopian traits were attributed were the Scythians, who inhabited the great plains of eastern Europe and western and central Asia. Accounts of them run through several centuries of Greek and Roman literature. Some are clearly mythological; others evidently record at first hand the visits of travelers. Since the name carried through a long period of time, and was applied to various tribes over a great extent of territory, it is not surprising that accounts vary greatly. One of the more utopian passages is by the Greek, Strabo, in his *Geography*, written in the first century B.C. He discusses the difference between Scythian tribes, some being cruel and others humane. Quoting Homer and Hesiod, he says of these people:

We consider them the simplest and the least crafty, and more thrifty and self-sufficient than we. And yet life in our manner has spread to almost all peoples a change for the worse, introducing luxury among them, and pleasures and evil practices and countless selfish acts. Hence much of this type of evil has penetrated to the Barbarians, to others as well as to the Nomads. . . .

Anacharsis and Abaris [who were Scythians] and certain others of this type were well thought of among the Greeks, because they showed the national character of good temper, plain-living, and justice. . . .

There are some of the Scythian Nomads who feed on mare's milk and in their justice surpass all, and the poets recall them to mind. Homer says, "The milk-drinking Abioi, the most righteous of men," speaking of Zeus looking down upon the land, and Hesiod in the so-called *Circuit of the Earth* says that Phineas was driven by the Harpies "into the land of the milk-drinkers who have houses on wagons." And he explains this on the ground that being thrifty and not business men, they are well-behaved towards one another, and have all things in common, their wives and children and their whole kin. Yet they are unconquerable by foreigners, for they have nothing for which they might be enslaved.[7]

Lovejoy and Boas, in their *Primitivism and Related Ideas in Antiquity*, have made a great contribution to our available knowledge of the subject. From the whole range of Greek and Roman literature they have assembled typical expressions, both of the tradition of the ages of mankind and presumed accounts of remote peoples with utopian traits. This work opens to English readers a treasury of classical material hitherto not generally accessible.

Theirs is a literary approach, and they adopt the view which has been general in modern times, attributing accounts of utopian traits among primitive peoples to sheer invention or to the gradual growth of myth and legend. Had they drawn upon the resources of anthropology as well, their views might have been somewhat modified. They might have reached the conclusion that without doubt many peoples have had strikingly utopian traits which very properly claim the admiration of men, and for this reason have become embedded in legend.

Compare what has been quoted concerning the Scythians with the following passages from Doughty's *Arabia Deserta*, in which this very observing traveler of a few decades ago describes conditions he found in remote parts of Arabia:

The nomad tribes we have seen to be commonwealths of brethren, ruled by their sheykhs with an equitable moderation. They divide each others' losses, and even in such there is community between whole tribes.

The malicious subtlety of usury is foreign to the brotherly dealing of the nomad tribesmen.

This is the council of the elders and the public tribunal. . . . Let him speak here who will, the voice of the least is heard among them. . . . Judgment is given commonly without partiality and always without bribes. . . . Their justice is such, that in the opinion of the next governed countries, the Arabs of the wilderness are the justest of mortals. Seldom the judge and elders err, in these small societies of kindred, where the life of every tribesman lies open from his infancy and his state is to all men well known.[8]

The authors of *Primitivism and Related Ideas in Antiquity* present the literature as reflecting two sharply conflicting doctrines, that of primitivism or the "noble savage," from which humanity has deteriorated, and antiprimitivism, the doctrine that primitive life was crude and unlovely, and that social excellence is the product of "civilization." Is it not realistic to see the course of human affairs to be a very mixed and complex pattern of advance and retrogression? The age-long difficulty in keeping these two doctrines separate may be due to the fact that each contains a measure of truth.

Lovejoy and Boas state: "At least from the fourth century B.C. on, then, the Scythians apparently were to the ancients very much what the North American Indians were to the primitivists of the sixteenth to the eighteenth centuries in modern Europe—except that, if anything, they were somewhat more realistically depicted than the American aborigines were." [9] Because sixteenth to eighteenth century writers took wide liberties in describing the traits of the "noble savages," it often has been assumed that opposite traits prevailed. Yet some of the more careful sociological studies of primitive societies during recent years indicate that very excellent social and personal traits are far from uncommon,[10] and often might contribute substantial elements to the design of a good society.

If we follow back the stories of utopian societies toward their origins we see how general is the habit of building on what had gone before, and how small in any case has been the element of sheer creative imagination. This is the case even with such masters of life, literature, and government as Plato, Thomas More, or Francis Bacon. These men proposed fundamental changes in society, it is true, but they did not to any large extent originate the ideas they presented.

In almost every case even the greatest of utopians inherited most of their seemingly novel ideas from those who had preceded them, their own contribution being in the way of refinements, additions, or better organization.

To assume that most legends of a well-ordered society are but wishful dreaming is to credit primitive people with unusual creative imagination. Does not such an assumption strain probability more than would a belief in the possibility of a historical basis for many of these legends?

That imagination and fantasy have entered into these traditions of the Golden Age, both in the original stories of travelers and by slow accretion through the generations, there is not a shadow of doubt. Every great religion which has survived for long periods has become loaded down with miracle and mythology; yet that is not adequate reason for denying the possibility of a core of fact as to its origin.

From certain other points of view, also, it seems much more reasonable to believe in the frequent existence of a Golden Age than in its nonexistence. When we carefully examine these ancient stories of a good society, such as Confucius' account of "The Grand Course," which is quoted later in this chapter, we find them to be, in effect, descriptions of a state of affairs in which men were well adjusted within themselves and in their relations with their neighbors. Men worked in unity, in harmony with each other, rather than in destructive friction or conflict.

Now good adjustment, either for a man or for a society, is a help to survival. Extreme and continued maladjustment tends to failure and elimination. It is a principle fully recognized by biologists and sociologists that in the process of evolution, whether of plants and animals, of men, or of human societies, there is a constant tendency for the process of selection to result in good adjustment. If an organism or a society is experiencing great disharmonies and destructive stresses, it is because through changes, either in its own organization or in its environment, the old harmonious adjustment has been destroyed.

From a purely scientific standpoint, therefore, we are justified in looking at extreme stress and disharmony in a society as representing a process of transition and attempted readjustment, as a passing, critical phase in the process of social evolution. In the one to six million or more years of existence attributed to the human species, during which primitive man lived in small, separate, nearly static communities, cases of long periods of relative stability, good adjustment, and internal harmony, such as are implied in legends of the Golden Age, would seem to be highly probable as a natural outcome of the evolutionary process.

Of the total existence of the human species, probably not more than one per cent is included in the historic period of almost constantly warring tribes, cities, and nations. Because the tragedy of maladjusted human life reaches back beyond the records of men, it seems endless; yet from the standpoint of evolution it may be but a short interlude, preceded by a long period in which stability and good adjustment were often achieved, with the present interlude probably to be followed by another long period of social harmony. To see the tragedy of man in its true setting one needs the sense of timing of the ancient poet who wrote, "A thousand years in thy sight are but as yesterday when it is past, and as a watch in the night."

The record of life on the earth is one of diversity rather than uniformity. To assume that there have been numerous extended cases or areas of fine social adjustment is not to claim that the entire human race had achieved such a status at any one time. Diversity in social adjustment is evident in the animal world. Some species of doves have achieved a high degree of internal social harmony, whereas the social order of the domestic fowl is a "peck order," based on dominance and coercion. The howler monkeys of Panama have a sort of utopian society, whereas other species of monkeys or apes are combative and tyrannous. Human societies have been similarly diverse in the development of social traits, though certain uniformities tend to emerge.

In exploring the evolution of human society we have access to evidence very similar to that which the biologist uses in the study of human evolution. Among the resources of the biologist are (1) comparative anatomy and physiology, (2) embryology, and (3) paleontology. In place of *comparative anatomy and physiology* the student of human evolution can observe the likenesses and differences of human societies, some of them survivors of ancient types still existing in out-of-the-way places. By observing the actual processes men follow in organizing themselves into societies, such as the social organization of New England or of the Mormons or of the vigilance committees during the California gold rush, we get hints of *social embryology*. It is an axiom of embryology that the individual in its development retraces the course of its evolution. In the fossils of extinct human societies embedded in a thousand ways in the structure of language, in proverbs, legends, fables, songs, and literature, in creeds, customs, and taboos, in our domesticated plants and animals, and in archeological remains, we may study *social paleontology*.

The writer is not qualified, nor is this the place, to outline a scientific study of the Golden Age. Yet he would like to drop a few hints, to expose a few fragments of evidence, and then to make a guess as to what might be the outcome of such a study.

A few years ago the scientific press announced the discovery off the east coast of Africa of a very primitive type of fish, of a class supposed to be long extinct. Students of animal evolution were intrigued by the opportunity to compare this living species with the ideas they had formed from fossils of extinct related species. Let us similarly compare a fossil of a society which was generally thought to be long extinct, or never to have existed outside of men's fancy, with a similar actual living society which has recently been discovered.

First let us look at what may be a fossil of an ancient society, found embedded in the ancient literature of China. Included in the writings of Confucius, but now supposed by some Oriental scholars to have another origin, perhaps even earlier, is the following description of a Golden Age:

"When the Grand Course was pursued, a public and a common spirit ruled all under the sky; they chose men of talents, virtue, and ability; their words were sincere, and what they cultivated was harmony. Thus men did not love their parents only, nor treated as children only their own sons. A competent provision was secured for the aged until their death, employment for the able-bodied, and the means of growing up to the young. They showed kindness and compassion to widows, orphans, childless men, and those who were disabled by disease, so that they were all sufficiently maintained. Males had their proper work, and females their homes. They accumulated articles of value, out of dislike that they should be wasted, but without any desire to keep them for their own gratification. They labored because they disliked not to use their strength, never solely for personal advantage. In this way selfish scheming was repressed, and found no development. Robbers, filchers, and rebellious traitors did not show themselves, and hence the outer doors remained open . . ." [11]

This legendary description might be considered as the fossil of an ancient society, thought to be long since extinct. But suppose that in some remote, nearly inaccessible, and almost unexplored corner of the earth, long separated from the rest of mankind, we should find a living society of Mongolians which in almost every respect corresponded to this ancient legend. Would we not get the same kind of thrill the scientists did who found a living fish of a family thought to be extinct?

Now the fact is that just such a Mongolian society has been found, and the few reports that have come to us concerning it are in general agreement as to its characteristics. Perhaps the clearest and most explicit description is that by Vilhjalmur Stefansson, the arctic explorer, who spent several years with the people of these communities northwest of Hudson Bay, and thoroughly learned their language. These Eskimos had not been in contact with white men, except when two or three arctic expeditions had penetrated their region during the past century, or possibly if they may have absorbed survivors of the pre-Columbian settlement of Greenland. Stefansson's accounts of these people who, he believes, came from the general region of China, are scattered through his several books. However, he has written a concise description of their society for his essay in the book, *I Believe*, edited by Clifton Fadiman. Stefansson's standing in his field gives authority to his account, a part of which is quoted here:

So far as my picture of the good life is derived from experience, I get it mainly from people of the Stone Age with whom I lived in the Coronation Gulf district of northern Canada.... from comparing ten years among savages with forty years in civilization ...

In culture the Gulf Eskimos went back not thousands but tens of thousands of years, for they were just emerging from the age of wood and horn into the earliest period of stone.

They had as much desire to live as any of us but less fear of dying than most of us.

Natural resources and raw materials were owned in common, but made articles were privately owned. The blubber of a seal that was needed for light and heat, or lean and fat that were needed for meals, belonged no more to the man who secured them than to anyone else. A pair of boots belonged to the woman who made them until she presented or sold them to somebody else. A meal that had been cooked was in a sense private property, but it was open to everyone under the laws of hospitality—it was very bad form to start a meal in any village without at the least sending a youngster outdoors to shout at the top of his voice that the family were about to dine or breakfast. . . . If the house was too small to accommodate everybody, then portions of cooked food were sent out to the other houses.

Among the Eskimos of northern Canada there was no law except public opinion. Although no one had authority, each person had influence according to the respect won from a community which had intimate knowledge of everybody. . . .

With the primitive Eskimos every debt was a debt of honor; for there were no police, judges, prisons, or punishment. . . .

The same force which compelled the Eskimo to pay his debts compelled him to do his share of the work according to his recognized abilities. I never knew even one who didn't try his best, although there were, of course, the same differences of energy and aptitude which we find among ourselves. If there had been a shirker, he would have received the same food; but, even in a circle of punctilious courtesy he would have felt that he was not being fed gladly. It is the nearest thing to impossible, when you know how primitive society works under communistic anarchy, to conceive of anyone with that combination of indolence and strength of character which would make it possible for a well man to remain long a burden on the community.

In the few cases where strength of character is enough for running against public opinion, the issue is seldom or never on any such low plane as that of indolence. I have known one situation where a man was condemned to death. For there was no punishment among the Stone Age Eskimos except the disapproval of the community, and death—nothing in between. [Stefansson states elsewhere that this case of death sentence resulted directly from the violation of the dignity and self-respect of an Eskimo by a white man, with the result that the Eskimo went wild.]

The worst crime, in the view of these anarchistic communists of the Stone Age, was troublemaking—indeed, there cannot be a more antisocial quality in a society that has no legal or punitive machinery. . . .

When the impression spreads, and is confirmed, that a certain person is a troublemaker, there begin informal discussions as to what should be done. . . . he may be warned by a relative or friend, the informer then expecting that the troublemaker will flee to a remote community. There have been cases, however, where he does not flee but begins to swagger, carrying weapons or having them handy day and night, defying everybody.

Theoretically the execution takes place only when the community is unanimous, and then it becomes the duty of the next of kin to be executioners. This prevents blood feuds . . .

Rank was determined by the things you secured and turned over to the common use. Your importance in the community depended on your judgment, your ability, and your character, but notably upon your unselfishness and kindness. Those who were useful to the community, who fitted well into the community pattern, were leaders.

. . . you don't have to accumulate food, apart from the community's store, for you are welcome to all you reasonably need of the best there is. You do not have to buy clothes, for they will be made for you . . . You do not have to own land where no one owns land; you do not own a house because no one owns houses, or wants to. You do not have to accumulate wealth against your old age, for the community will support you as gladly when you are too old to work as it would if you had never been able to work at all—say because you had been blind from childhood.

Fortunately we do not have to debate whether little-civilized and uncivilized Eskimos are the happiest people in the world, for most travelers have agreed on their being the happiest, or at least seeming to be. . . .

On the basis of my years with the people of the Age of Stone, I feel my vote will have to be that . . . the chief factor in the happiness of the Stone Age Eskimos was that they were living according to the golden rule.

In the Stone Age community those who were selfish lost standing. Those who were altruistic rose in the public esteem. A man who got things to use them himself was not frowned on so long as everybody felt that what he was using was not beyond his needs; but whenever anyone began to keep for himself more than by the usual experience was necessary for his comfort, he lost some of the community's good opinion; if he gave the impression that his main purpose for getting things was that he wanted to keep them, then he fell in standing rapidly. However, that situation never went far, in my experience, for I never actually knew anybody who had the "moral" courage to persist in the acquisitive type of unsocial conduct.[12]

We have mentioned that nearly three thousand years ago Homer sang utopian songs of the men at the ends of the earth, the Hyperboreans (men who lived back of the north wind) and the Aethiopians, far toward the south. In the description by Stefansson we have a recent report from true Hyperboreans. To avoid partiality we shall include a description of "Aethiopians," at the far extreme of the Dark Continent. P. Kolben, in *The Present State of the Cape of Good Hope*, gives us such an account:

In Munificence and Hospitality the *Hottentots*, perhaps go beyond all other nations upon earth. They love and pleasure and relieve one another with such a noble Simplicity and Largeness of Heart as I have never met with among all the other peoples I have seen.... Father Tachart says well: "The *Hottentots* have more Honesty, Love and Liberality for One another than are almost anywhere seen among Christians...." I have seen the very things he mentions again and again. And I know that when a *Hottentot* does but catch a little Venison, or a Dish of Fish, he invites his neighbors to dine with him upon it; and everyone is welcome as far as the treat will go.

And all of them trade and transact with one another at all Times in the most upright and friendly Manner; as they do likewise with the *Europeans*, whenever the latter are upon the Square.[13]

While this account seems very laudatory, it occurs in a description of the Hottentots in which their shortcomings, as in diet habits or lack of personal cleanliness, are stated boldly and without hesitation. Kropotkin, after discussing the Hottentots, states in his *Mutual Aid*, in reference to their gentleness and kindness, "These very same words have been applied to the Ostyaks, the Samoyedes, the Eskimos, the Dayaks, the Aleoutes, the Papuas, and so on, by the highest authorities."

To indicate further the world-wide distribution of well-adjusted societies among primitive peoples we may turn to the tropical Arapesh of New Guinea, as described from her personal observations by Dr. Margaret Mead, Director of Ethnology of the American Museum of Natural History:

All economic activities [of the Arapesh] are conducted in small groups which work together in terms of personal ties between members and without more than lip service to the clan structure. Each man is a member of from two to six working groups...

The fortunate man, who thinks he has a large surplus [of yams], will consult his elders, or they themselves may tell him that his supply is sufficient. He then gathers all his yams in one place ... and after he and a series of associates—brothers, cousins, brother-in-law, etc.—have gathered together enough meat, he gives a large feast to which most of the locality come, and members of adjacent and related hamlets. Each guest family brings gifts, mainly meat, but also net bags, plates, etc., and takes away a part of the piled up yams to use as seed, seed from which the maker of the abullu can never eat again. He has the honor of having given the abullu ... and his gardening luck has increased the food supply of the community. Although this is always phrased positively—that a man is "permitted" to make an abullu—it is actually an effective measure against any one man's accumulating wealth disproportionate to the wealth accumulated by others.

If there is meat on his smoking rack over the fire, it is either meat which was killed by another ... and has been given to him, in which case he and his family may eat it; or it is meat which he himself has killed and which he is smoking to give away to someone else, for to eat one's own kill, even though it be only a small bird, is a crime to which only the morally—which usually means in Arapesh mentally—deficient will stoop. If the house in which he is living is nominally his, it will have been constructed in part at least from the posts and planks of other people's houses, which have been dismantled or temporarily deserted, and from which he has borrowed timber. He will not cut his rafters to fit his house, if they are too long, because they may be needed later for someone else's house which is of a different shape or size.

The Arapesh ideal man is one who shows an all-round capacity for devotion to the community ends, one who is able and willing to lead in spite of a native dislike for leadership, one who is hospitable, wise, gentle, unquarrelsome, and intelligent in the sense that he is able to understand the ends of his society and to carry them out.... Such a man is valued far above the man who shows special skills.

The community has very few well-developed sanctions, partly because there is no concept that proper social behavior is difficult or that it needs to be enforced.

Fighting between little children is never permitted.... Over and over again the point is made that one may injure oneself if one wishes, but one must not hurt others.

The Arapesh are a society within which cooperation toward a general cherishing conserving goal is obtained through the ramification of helpfulness within person-to-person ties rather than by any allegiance to closed groups or by any resort to rivalry or competition between groups. The multiplicity of these person-to-person ties prevents any boundaries being set up either to the groups

with common language, which are crosscut with trade relationships, to the localities, which are crosscut with affinal, residence,
and working-group ties, or to the biological family itself, so close
are the ties of each spouse to the relatives of the other. Conspicuous also is the diffuseness of the goal set up by the society, the
number of ways in which a satisfactory functioning may be at-
tained, the freedom left to the individual to choose or reject a
skill, the lack of any single scale by which success can be
measured.[14]

In many, many cases, in all parts of the world and in
many periods of history, small human societies in varying
degrees have achieved a condition of social harmony, of
which we have numerous fragmentary records. For instance,
Thomas Morton, writing about 1637, less than twenty years
after the first settlement of Massachusetts, said of the Indians
in that region, ". . . their life is so void of care, and they
are so loving also that they make use of those things they
enjoy (the wife of one excepted), as common goods, and
are therein so compassionate that, rather than one should
starve through want, they would starve all." [15] Kropotkin's
Mutual Aid includes summaries of many such records.

Many of the most treasured ideals of men today seem to
be, not recent inventions, but survivals and resurgences of
ancient ways which in spite of a long period of feudalism
and empire held their own in remote or sheltered places, or
close to the soil, to spring up again when the environment
was more favorable. The Christian ethic was not a sudden
revelation, but came down through the centuries, kept alive
in the small communities of Palestine and preserved in the
messages of the Hebrew prophets, until it was carried to
the world in the Christian movement. How closely it re-
sembles the ancient Eskimo ethic!

The earliest of the Hebrew prophets whose message has
survived was Amos, who described himself as a herdsman

and a gatherer of sycamore fruits—a man of a rural community. Except for the very important elements of making brotherhood world-wide instead of community-wide and of making forgiveness unlimited, the Golden Rule and the Sermon on the Mount were not a new revelation, but a restatement of very old social principles. Were they not survivals of a Golden Age of community life?

Switzerland has been like a beacon light to the world, showing the way to democracy. Yet democracy was no recent Swiss invention. When, seven hundred years ago, the men of the three forest cantons made their covenant of everlasting union, defeated the feudal army, and tore down the baron's castle, they were not inventing democracy. They were but defending the ancient democratic way of life described in Caesar's *Gallic War* and in Tacitus's *History of the Germans*, a way of living that through the centuries in the Alpine valleys had escaped the grasping tentacles of feudalism.

The thousand-year-old Icelandic parliament, said to be the oldest democratic legislative body in existence, also inherited its vitality from community ways of still earlier times. These had survived because in Scandinavia feudalism had not completely submerged democracy. The organization of nineteenth- and twentieth-century Denmark was consciously and deliberately built on a revival of the ancient Danish folkways, largely through the efforts of Dr. Grundtvig, father of the Danish folk schools. The stubbornly persistent democracy of Sweden, Norway, and Finland has a similar history.

The democratically governed branches of the Christian church also hark back to an ancient lineage. As political feudalism overran Europe, Asia, and North Africa, nearly everywhere eliminating democratic processes in political life, so the Roman Empire, taking on the mantle of the Christian faith, in the guise of authoritative religion, destroyed or submerged primitive democratic religion. The divine right of the head of the state and the divine right of the head of the church were but two expressions of the same doctrine. It is significant that democracy in religion emerged into renewed prominence in the same sheltered or isolated spots where feudalism had not destroyed primitive communal and democratic life. The Waldensians, in constant danger of extermination by intolerance, in their high Alpine retreats clung for many centuries to a way of life much like that described in stories of the Golden Age. They influenced other areas where similar traditions had not been extinguished. It was no accident that Zwingli, who far outran Luther in making the reformation democratic, came from free peasants in a Swiss mountain community. His ancestors never had surrendered to feudalism.

The Swiss Anabaptists, who fully defined the modern doctrine of a free church in a free state, also grew out of that ancient tradition. Their doctrines had the widest acceptance in Scandinavia and close to the soil in England, where feudalism had not wholly extinguished the ancient ways. The "Twelve Articles" of the German peasants, of the year 1525, were not the initial expression of the doctrines they advanced. Rather, the peasants were making a last stand for a very old communal democracy. As the "Twelve Articles" indicate, the people intuitively recognized the identity of the primitive Christian way of life with their own.

With the slaughter of a hundred thousand of their number in the ensuing Peasants' Revolt their ancient ways seemed to be definitely destroyed; yet they continued to re-emerge in the religious democracy of the Baptists, Friends, Mennonites, Unitarians, and other followings, while their political democracy still stirs the hearts of men. More than most groups, the Mennonites have deliberately maintained a continuous tradition of political and religious freedom and of community life. Even in the individualistic, commercial atmosphere of America the ancient pattern of a Golden Age still finds spontaneous expression among some branches of the Mennonites in their many co-operative undertakings, both formal and informal.

Thus in bits of living society and in historical records we find vestiges of ways of life substantially like those preserved in many legends of a Golden Age. It does not follow that the biological and social adjustment which characterized much of primitive community life was faultless. Associated with the community spirit, the mutual respect and regard, the co-operative mutual effort for common ends, which were precious common elements of very many communities, there was a darker side. Primitive societies, regardless of the sincerity and good will of their members, had marked disadvantages. In the universal human effort to discover laws and principles to explain their experiences, mistakes were often made, and mistaken theories were developed. As a result, these primitive societies often labored under a burden of superstitions, taboos, false dogmas, blood feuds, and erratic philosophies. Frazer's *Golden Bough* is a classic record of such inhibitions. Yet many primitive societies were relatively free from taboos and mythology.

Primitive communities were also very helpless before nature. Famine, flood, and pestilence often mastered them. They lacked that security against natural calamity which the modern world has so largely achieved.

As a result of limiting associations to small numbers, usually of one's own small group, and from lack of travel and intellectual cross-fertilization, primitive communities tended to be narrowly provincial. Their social codes often were ill-adjusted to a world of constant change. Men of Golden Age communities often lived and thought according to the prevailing pattern, and in some cases knew little of intellectual freedom. However, it was in the little city-states and small island communities of Greece, more than in the great empires of the Nile and the Euphrates, that critical world views emerged.

While there was a high degree of good will within the primary group, intercommunity feuds were frequent. The Christian doctrine of the brotherhood of all men, which is essential to complete the pattern of a good life, was missing. These little societies were too small to fulfill the possibilities of human destiny. No sane person will uncritically approve *in toto* the ways of any Golden Age society, nor wish for their undiscriminating reinstatement. Yet, at least in numerous cases, those long ages of small communities had achieved and had deeply established in the texture of primary human societies certain great and ideal traits which men everywhere recognize as adding to the value of human living. The new Golden Age will recapture the qualities of good will, mutual respect and confidence, intimate acquaintance, and co-operative endeavor; but it will add to them the spirit of free inquiry, mastery of the physical environment, eugenic improvement of the race, and a wide cosmopolitan range of cultural interests. The problem of the utopian has ever been, not uncritically to reproduce the Golden Age, but to recapture its values, and to give them a larger and more universal setting.

With the suggestion that the concept of the Golden Age in actual societies of the past be recovered from the realm of mythology and given serious study from an anthropological as well as from a literary point of view, let the writer venture a guess as to what such a study might disclose. When any small human community lives for a long period undisturbed from the outside, a prophylactic or hygienic process takes place within it. The community tends to eliminate antisocial members, and to purge itself from antisocial habits and attitudes. Men come to be known for what they actually are. Because of that intimate acquaintance, candor wins out over falsehood, sincerity displaces duplicity. When men come to know each other thoroughly, then, to use the utopian expression of Isaiah, "The vile person shall be no more called liberal, nor the churl said to be bountiful." In small, isolated communities the world over, human nature has a tendency to develop certain qualities that claim our respect and admiration.

Among the earlier writings of Edward Bellamy is a fanciful story entitled "To Whom This May Come," in which he gives his impression of the effect which complete and intimate acquaintance would have upon personal character and social relations. The characters in the story are descendants of some Persian mystics who were shipwrecked two thousand years ago on an isolated island. During the centuries they had become able to read each other's minds completely. The following passages indicate the refining influence which the author pictures as resulting from full mutual understanding:

...the very knowledge that my mind was overlooked by others operated to check thoughts that might be painful to them, and that, too, without more effort of the will than a kindly person exerts to check the utterance of disagreeable remarks. As a very few lessons in the elements of courtesy cures a decent person of inconsiderate speaking, so a brief experience among the mind-readers went far in my case to check inconsiderate thinking.... among the mind-readers, politeness never can extend to the point of insincerity, as among talking nations, seeing that it is always one another's real and inmost thought that they read.... For the very reason that the mind-reader reads all your thoughts, particular thoughts are judged with reference to the general tenor of thought. Your characteristic and habitual frame of mind is what he takes account of. No one need fear being misjudged by a mind-reader on account of sentiments or emotions which are not representative of the real character or general attitude.

.... the very completeness of the disclosure of my thoughts and motives was a guarantee that I would be judged with a fairness and a sympathy such as even self-judgment cannot pretend to, affected as that is by so many subtle reactions.... How shall I describe the delightful exhilaration of moral health and cleanness, the breezy oxygenated mental condition, which resulted from the consciousness that I had absolutely nothing concealed! ... What stronger testimony could there be to the instinctive consciousness that concealment is debauching, and openness our only cure, than the world-old conviction of the virtue of confession for the soul, and that the uttermost exposing of one's worst and foulest is the first step toward moral health? ... think what health and soundness there must be for souls among a people who see in every face a conscience which, unlike their own, they cannot sophisticate, who confess one another with a glance, and shrive with a smile! ... though ages may elapse before the slow event shall justify me ... in no way will the mutual vision of minds, when at last it shall be perfected, so enhance the blessedness of mankind as by rending the veil of self, and leaving no spot of darkness in the mind for lies to hide in.

... mind-reading is chiefly held desirable, not for the knowledge of others which it gives its possessors, but for the self-knowledge which is its reflex effect.... Every one must needs always think of himself as he is, being no more able to do otherwise than is a man in a hall of mirrors to cherish delusions as to his personal appearance.

Among a people who are compelled by the very constitution of their minds to put themselves in the places of others, the sympathy which is the inevitable consequence of perfect comprehension renders envy, hatred, and uncharitableness impossible.[16]

This story by Bellamy pictures the absolute stage of a process which tends to take place in a small community in which people are intimately acquainted.

In the Chinese collection of utopian sketches, the *Ching*

Hua Yüan, or "Flowers in the Mirror," which is mentioned in the chapter on "The Origins of Utopia," there is a charming utopian fantasy, "The Country of Great Men," which treats of this same theme of the good results which would follow if all the members of society should fully understand each other's innermost character and motives. A few quotations will illustrate the manner in which the theme of Bellamy's story "To Whom This May Come" was dealt with half a century before in China:

A voyage of a few days brought them to the Country of Great Men, where they would hardly have landed but for T'ang's curiosity to see a people who he had heard used clouds as a means of locomotion.... the city lay at some distance from the shore behind a range of hills ... So they set off to walk, meeting on the way a few people moving about on clouds of different colours about half a foot from the ground ... They spied out a small temple hidden in a grove of waving bamboos, and were on the point of knocking for admittance, when out came an old man ...
... T'ang prayed him to excuse them ... He then added, "May I ask what is the explanation of the clouds I see underneath the feet of the inhabitants of this country? Are you born with them?"

"Sir," answered the old priest, "these clouds are perfectly independent of the will of the individuals to whom they are attached. Their colour varies, and also changes, with the disposition of each particular person. The best clouds to have are striped like a rainbow; yellow is the second best, and black is the worst of all." ... our travellers forthwith proceeded on their way ... all the inhabitants were moving about on clouds of various hues, green, red, yellow, blue, and black. Amongst others they noticed a filthy beggar riding on a striped or rainbow cloud; whereupon T'ang remarked, "Why, the priest told us that the striped cloud was the best of all, and here is a dirty old beggar with one!"

"When I was here before," explained Tou Chiu-kung, "I heard that the colour of a man's cloud was quite independent of his wishes, being regulated entirely by his natural disposition and actions, so that virtuous people shew good colours and wicked people bad ones whether they like or not; and that nothing short of change of disposition and conduct can possibly alter the hue of any man's cloud. Thus it happens that persons of high rank are sometimes seen on black clouds, while their poorer and humbler neighbors ride about on clouds of the very best colours. As it is, I would have you notice how few—scarcely two in a hundred— are seen on black clouds. For such are held in universal detestation by their fellow-countrymen, who avoid contact with them as much as they can; whereas, on the other hand, nothing gives more pleasure to the inhabitants of this region than the sight of a kindly and benevolent act. Neither are they always striving to get the better of one another, and therefore the people of the adjacent nations have named this the country of great men; not meaning thereby that physically speaking they are greater than the usual run of human beings, but that they are a high-minded and virtuous race."

Suddenly there was a cleavage in the throng of pedestrians and an official came down the street dressed in a black, round-collared coat and black hat followed by an attendant holding a red umbrella over his head. The wreath of cloud beneath his feet was covered by a piece of red silk.

"That official evidently requires no carriage with that cloud to carry him along," remarked T'ang. "But why cover it up with a piece of silk?"

"That official is like a man who stops his ears to steal a string of bells," said Chiu-kung. "It is futile, of course, to try to conceal the color of his cloud. Everybody knows that the cloud has turned grey, or perhaps black because the rider has done something against his own conscience. Fortunately, the color can be changed by sincere repentance; otherwise, not only would the official be punished by the King, but he would be ostracized by all the inhabitants." [17]

The results assumed by Bellamy and described in "The Country of Great Men" are strikingly similar to conditions actually found by Stefansson and other visitors to remote Eskimo communities. Many small religious societies, such as the Waldensians, the Friends, and the Mennonites, have maintained as groups a high level of conduct, partly because they acted as compact communities with definite standards of living.

When communities grow large, and people cannot thoroughly and intimately know each other, some of the better qualities of the cultural inheritance survive only with difficulty, for duplicity may prevail over sincerity, selfishness may win out over social-mindedness. Machiavelli in *The Prince* gave classic expression to this changed basis for social control:

> ... as the generality of mankind are wicked, and ever ready to break their words, a prince should not pique himself in keeping his more scrupulously, especially as it is always easy to justify a breach of faith on his part.... It is necessary, however, to disguise the appearance of craft, and thoroughly to understand the art of feigning and dissembling; for men are generally so simple and so weak, that he who wishes to deceive easily finds dupes.
>
> Pope Alexander VI. played during his whole life a game of deception; and ... his artifices always proved successful.... This was because he so well understood this chapter in the art of government.... A prince should ... never ... utter anything which does not breathe of kindness, justice, good faith, and piety: this last quality it is most important for him to appear to possess, as men in general judge more from appearances than from reality.... Every one sees your exterior, but few can discern what you have in your heart ...

Gracian, the Spanish Jesuit, also saw as a "realist" when he wrote, "Know how to let the blame slip upon another:

to have a shield against malevolence is wise strategy on the part of those who govern, a thing not born of weakness ... but of greater strength ..." [18] And also, "All that gains approval, do yourself, and all that gains disapproval through another." [19]

The Golden Age began to fade when, with the conquest of some communities by others, or through the coalescence of small communities into larger, life became so complex or numbers so great that intimate acquaintance no longer was possible; therefore duplicity, sham, and other forms of deceit would succeed in practice. Men who have grown up in an atmosphere of good faith and then have to deal with those who explicitly and deliberately follow the Machiavellian code, find themselves greatly handicapped. In time, deep indoctrination of selfishness, shrewdness, and duplicity, and the resulting cowardice in the ranks of the people, come to be identified with human nature.

This tendency is accelerated by warfare, for under conditions of warfare deceit, suspicion, and brutality seem to be more useful traits than sincerity and good will. War is the greatest destroyer of the traits which I have ascribed to "Golden Age" cultures. Communities in regions which for long periods have been the battlegrounds of empires often give the impression that human nature is of a very low order. Where military conquest is followed by servitude of the vanquished, conditions necessary for the survival of dignity and refinement of personality may be largely destroyed.

The process by which small societies began to coalesce into larger units is not fully known. Most ancient civilizations began in irrigated regions. Quite probably the physical necessity for co-operating in larger groups to build reservoirs and canals that were beyond the reach of any one community was one cause of enlarged societies. Or the conquest of a rich and soft valley community by a hard and vigorous hill community, facing starvation after drouth, may have brought consolidation into larger social units. It was perhaps in such ways that the feudal process began.

As feudal lords seized control of society they did not at once change the intimate ancestral community culture. Close to the soil there continued neighborliness, co-operativeness, mutual confidence, good will, and affection, which had been developing in primitive communities for hundreds of thousands of years. In fact, these traits still continue to be the actual foundation qualities of human society. They constitute the cement which holds society together and the energy which gives it life.

It is only because a residue of the Golden Ages lives and grows in men's spirits and in community ways that organized society continues to exist. Vice would not imitate virtue, duplicity would not appear as sincerity, if better qualities were not present and in high regard among men, and so worth imitating. A parasite can thrive only so long as its host remains alive. With the death of the Golden Age in the spirits of men, society would disintegrate. The decline and death of great nations and cultures may be explained by the decline of "Golden Age" qualities under the impact of power politics and the regime of force and shrewdness. Fortunately, the Golden Age has had many seed-beds, from the hills of Galilee to the icy shores of Baffin-Land, and in numberless homes and neighborhoods, from which it may spread again among men.

The fine qualities which have characterized many small communities often have been thought of as rural traits, not suitable to large aggregations of men. The socialist or utopian is not likely to strengthen his case for a reorganization of society by pointing to these tiny units. In Europe and Asia the growth of large states has taken place not so much by the expansion and extension of ancient community ways as by

overriding or ignoring them. As a result it has become almost
an axiom of European and Asiatic political thought that
"brotherhood economics," though perhaps desirable in the
provincial atmosphere of the village, has no place in large-
scale political policy, where cynical self-interest must control.

In Peru, on the contrary, the mutual helpfulness of small
community groups was not abandoned in the process of
empire building, but was carried over and made the dominant
characteristic of the structure of states and of a great empire.
That structure resulted in vast technical developments, an
immense increase in the physical resources for living, an unprecedented degree of economic security, and a high level
of loyalty and good will toward the government. When that
structure was broken down from without by the circumstances
we have described, and the Asiatic-European pattern took its
place, there followed a general deterioration of the vast technical works, a great shrinkage of physical resources and of
population, and a general and long continued demeaning of
life of the mass of the people. Dominance by the imposition
of force is not final proof of inherent human excellence.

Does not this course of events suggest that the age-long
self-seeking, exploiting, impoverishing political and social
pattern of Europe and Asia is not an inevitable and universal
social imperative, but rather is the pattern which particular
circumstances imposed on a continental culture? Had the
"Golden Age" traits of primitive communities by fortunate
chance been incorporated into the process of nation-building
in Europe and Asia, as it was in ancient western South
America, might not the history of the great continent have
been finer and happier?

I have expressed a supposition of how the Golden Age
was almost lost as a controlling pattern of society. How can
it be regained? Not by naively protesting that "honesty is
the best policy," but by trying to create a society in which
that shall be the case. That undertaking, in effect, is the

burden of the utopians. For it to be successful changes of
several kinds are required. First, there must be refinement
of the personal impulses and motivations. To recover such
refinement under existing conditions may require greater
stamina and skill than would be necessary simply to maintain it in the Golden Age. It requires the elimination of
antisocial and other unethical indoctrination, and the development of personal habits which promote social harmony and
well-being.

Next, it is essential to modify the formal structure of
society, economics, and government, so that they will favor
and not penalize ethical action and social motives. Men must
be educated to distinguish between sincerity and sham in
social behavior, and must provide better ways for making
true appraisals of personal qualities.

Lastly, for any of these changes to succeed fully and
permanently, it is necessary to develop a general understanding and application of the science of eugenics.

Most utopians have believed it is possible to organize the
social and economic structure so that wholesome impulses
will be ascendant. Men of religion at their best have emphasized the need for so refining human character and motives
that they will bring about a better social structure. Educators
have urged the training of understanding, so that action can
be effective. All these approaches are mutually essential, as
in the use of steam power the force of steam, the mechanical
device of the steam engine, and the intelligent management
of the operator are mutually necessary in order that useful
work may be done.

As a Golden Age is achieved again, it may be more un-
alloyed than any in the past. In Edward Bellamy's description of utopia in his last book, *Equality*, we read, "The priestly
idea that the past was diviner than the present . . . gave place
to the belief that we should look forward and not backward
for inspiration . . ." [20] A greater knowledge of the life of

ancient man might have led him to get encouragement from both directions.

To discover that many legends of the Golden Age are founded on historical circumstances, and are not merely mythological creations of the human fancy, should give greater courage to believe that human nature of itself is not inconsistent with a good society.

When Fénelon was educating the ill-fated heir to the French throne, one of his methods was to write his famous utopia, *Telemachus*. At the conclusion of that work he pictures Minerva giving her parting advice to Telemachus, son of Ulysses. When she has completed his education, guiding him about the world in her disguise as a teacher, she tells him: "When thou shalt be invested with sovereign power, let it be thy only ambition to restore the Golden Age." In America, where every man is sovereign, what more pertinent counsel could be given?

VII

Characteristics and Use of Utopias

W E HAVE DRAWN NO NARROW BOUNDARIES for the utopian theme. Any picture or pattern which has gone beyond current achievement in presenting the possibilities of a good society has been considered within the range of interest. Some such writings are in the twilight zone between utopia and philosophy, as for instance, Plato's *Republic*.

In the marginal zone between utopia and government are numerous treatises which fall into one class or the other depending on circumstances or outlook. The biblical book of Deuteronomy is looked upon by some as a utopian picture of a good society, by others as a code of laws that to a considerable degree was actually lived by. The idealized code drafted in the cabin of the *Mayflower* during the long slow months of the passage overseas, which breathed the spirit of Watt Tyler, has come to be considered utopian.

Joseph Smith, a Vermont boy, in all probability a *Mayflower* descendant, and with some of the *Mayflower* spirit in him, outlined a political and social code which seemed strongly utopian. Yet the brotherhood which the boy had planned did come into existence; and, under the forceful leadership of his successors, three quarters of a million Mormons maintain a highly significant pattern of social and economic organization, and have made the desert bloom as the rose. Our federal Constitution, if it had not worked out successfully, would have been called utopian. Having succeeded in large degree it is practical government with us, whereas in certain Latin American countries, where it was copied but did not work, it is utopian.

An interesting case of a social pattern which was at one time a program of actual government, and later a utopia, is "The Memorial of a Myriad Words," which was produced by the Chinese statesman Wang An Shih in A.D. 1058, and which under the emperor Jin Tsung was the actual program of a "new deal" government for twenty years. Thereafter it was repudiated by a reactionary regime, its adherents were eliminated, and almost every copy of the document was destroyed. Long afterward two copies were found, one of them sealed up in the brick wall of a house. Through the centuries it has existed as a utopian dream.

In the region between ethics and religion, on the one hand, and utopia, on the other, we find similar indefiniteness of boundary. The Hebrew prophets, followed by the bearer of a message of world brotherhood, and St. Augustine and his *City of God*, all have been classified in both fields.

So we might continue our list of those writings that are in the no-man's-land between utopia and other fields. We might inquire whether Rousseau and his *Social Contract*, and Harrington and his *Oceana*, were utopians or authors of treatises on political philosophy. We might wonder whether the utopian spirit or the spirit of satire for its own sake is dominant in Aristophanes' *Ecclesiazusae*, Swift and his Gulliver, Butler and his *Erewhon*, and Voltaire and his *Zadig*. The same question might be asked about the Chinese travel tales, "Flowers in the Mirror."

Even in works of fiction utopian elements appear. We find them in Defoe's *Robinson Crusoe* and in the large number of imitators known as "Robinsons," the best known among them being *The Swiss Family Robinson* and, in German, *Insel Felsenburg*. We may even trace utopian features in such "pure" fantasies as Jules Verne's *Twenty Thousand Leagues Under the Sea* and E. Rider Haggard's *King Solomon's Mines*. The great Shakespeare could not resist playing about the margins of utopia, as in *The Tempest* and *As You Like It*. Occasionally a man like H. G. Wells ranges all around the borders of utopia, through religion, philosophy, government, and economics, to adventure and pure fantasy.

Should a commission of the wisest men be set up to define exactly the boundaries of utopia, they must fail; for no sooner would they turn their backs than some intrepid people would put some utopian scheme to work and bring it into the domain of practical life. Why, then, should the author trouble himself about whether he has ignored the proper boundaries of his subject? The author has not so troubled himself. Wherever the utopian theme appears, in whatever form of literature, he has considered it to be within his domain. Not content with this liberty, he has added mention of another region, in a concluding chapter, "Beyond Utopia."

When a man makes a garden or builds a house or a city, be begins to express a design of orderly arrangement—to make his work conform to a preconceived pattern. Almost every single item in our vast and complex American civilization was first a design in some man's mind before it was worked out into reality. The quality of our civilization is the quality of those designs. Occasionally there are men in whom this sense of design extends its range of action until it achieves an inclusive view of life as a whole in all its relationships. A description of such an inclusive view, especially if it is in the form of a picture of an ideal society as though it actually existed, may properly be called a utopia.

Every intelligent and active-minded person is to some degree a utopian. In our leisure moments we try to picture to ourselves the political, social and technical conditions under which we should like to live, and, at least in some small degree, we try to realize those conditions. The process of uncritical trying of this and that to see whether it will work is better than completely inert conservatism, at least as regards simple circumstances. However, in complex situations the wrong ways may so vastly outnumber the right ones, that the prospect of success by unsystematic, impulsive experiment may be very, very remote. The results of that type of experiment are chiefly waste of resources, disillusionment, and the discrediting of creative effort.

Up to the present, much of political and social experiment has been of that uncritical, impulsive character. Where the total resources and energies of great nations are involved in such experiments, the process is exceedingly wasteful and dangerous. Repeatedly the people have had high hopes, only to have them dashed to the ground; and such will continue to be common experience except to the extent that a new method of social pioneering becomes general. The new social process, of critical analysis and of orderly, creative design disciplined by the results of such analysis, makes possible a great reduction of risk and waste in making social changes, and promises greater and more rapid achievement.

The process of critical inquiry and analysis, with orderly design controlled by established principles and pertinent facts, is called engineering. Only as a similar process comes to prevail in the field of human relations will the conditions of society greatly improve. The social engineer is imperative.

The engineer does not dispense with the use of imagination or intuition. He is as much artist as he is analyst. He does not build from nothing. He begins with suggestions from his experience, or from the designs of others, or from imagination. He must have mental pictures of possible solutions before he can analyze and test and compare. The more nearly he is equipped with mental pictures of all possible solutions to his problem, the greater is the probability that he will reach the best possible result.

So it is with the social engineer. His is not an abstract mathematical process. He should have mental pictures of all possible solutions of his problem, so that in the process of analysis, test, and comparison, no significant prospect may be overlooked. Utopias are among the chief sources of suggestion for the social engineer. At their best they represent the essence of the world's thought regarding the possibilities of human society.

Most suggestions of design which are helpful to an engineer come from men who are disciplined and experienced in their field. Similarly, most utopias of any value are the work of intelligent and imaginative men who have been active participants or disciplined observers of affairs. They are by no means the work of idle dreamers.

The two general reasons why human societies do not reach perfection have already been suggested. One is that, like the trees in the forest, different societies crowd each other, trying to win "a place in the sun," and also are thwarted, injured, and blighted by flood, famine, pestilence, and other adverse natural circumstances. The other reason for social imperfection is no less important. Unlike a tree of the forest, human society is without a single common, definite pattern of growth, or idea or ideal. In an anthill there apparently is no rebellion or internal discord. The prevailing type of social organization is completely recognized and accepted. In human society no such fixed social pattern exists. Fortunately men are still free to explore the vast ranges of possible social organization and to work out new designs as human experience and insight increase, or as conditions of living change.

Much of the discord, grief, and conflict in the world today is the result, not of men's inability to achieve social aims, but of the absence of agreement concerning social aims on which to unite their efforts. When we observe how far from agreement on a social program those men are who are ablest in the field of government and social organization, we realize that it is not yet time for any single type of government to be fixed on society. The existence of disagreement and conflict, and the lack of unity of inner impulse toward achieving an ideal design, are not necessarily a hopeless or even an undesirable condition. Such discord indicates that society is in active evolution and is feeling its way toward larger and better patterns. We are as yet in the dim morning twilight of social science. Premature unity might result in fixing on society an unnecessarily imperfect type.

For a design for society to find expression in the actual structure of society and of government there is necessary a vast expenditure of life and resources, no small part of which expenditure at present is made in efforts to eliminate competing designs. The world today is in the throes of conflict between competitive utopias that are struggling for realization. Each of the social philosophies now fighting for self-preservation or for dominance is presented to the peoples who live under it as ideal and as suitable for universal application. Each one is a product of tradition and experience, combined with partly untested theory. Each one is in some respects so crude and imperfect as to raise doubts about whether it should become dominant, at least until further evolution and development have taken place. However, there is scarcely one of these social philosophies which does not include wholesome and desirable elements which might be universally adopted with profit.

If each of these social philosophies were being held by a people tentatively, with open minds, and with the aim of correcting and refining it, but not with the purpose of imposing it on others, then the resulting variety would be enlightening and stimulating. In the process of critical examination, comparison, and refinement the excellences of each system of social organization would emerge, and weaknesses would become evident and could be removed.

When a people is taught to hold its social philosophy, not tentatively and open-mindedly, but as the finally best form of society which all the world must sometime accept, then destructive competition and conflict follow, of which the recent world war is an example. While Americans are passionately, emotionally loyal to the name of democracy, its actual operation in our own political life is seen to be very imperfect, and relatively few people are wholly committed to it in practice. The best outcome of the recent world war would not be the imposition upon the world of what we call democracy, but the emergence of an attitude of mutual tolerance for different types of social organization. Our utopias should have only tentative adoption and use on a limited scale until they can be thoroughly examined, tested, and criticized. In the end it is by practical results and not only by theory that they must be judged.

Therefore the great social need today is not that men shall agree on a single type of social organization, but that they shall come to recognize principles of integrity, mutual respect, tolerance, and local autonomy combined with interdependence, which will make possible a continuing process of social experiment and exploration without destructive conflict. The colossal waste of life and resources which takes place in the competive struggle for a pattern of government, both by class and party struggles within nations and by war between nations, might be largely eliminated if men but realized that they are blindly feeling their way toward a good organization of society. With tolerance, patience, and good will; with free inquiry and aggressive exploration; with absence of dogmatism and without reliance on revelation or panacea, unprecedented progress might be made. Instead of a spirit of desperation and hatred—of fighting for life—there might be the zest and interest of exploration and adventure. Should such a change of social feeling once take place, any thought of reverting to present methods of violent competition would be looked upon as insanity. No change of human nature is needed, but only a change in the "conditioning" of the human spirit.

Pictures of a good life that have come to us range all the way from the daydreams of unrestrained wishful thinking to appeals for rigorous discipline and reconstruction of life as essential preparation for a better day. At one extreme, only the rubbing of Aladdin's magic lamp is necessary to turn a shiftless ne'er-do-well into an opulent prince. In contrast is the prophet Amos, calling for a radical reformation of life and character as essential to any real hope for his people. Some of the Arabian Nights stories seem to have come down from a remote past. It may be that in the light of the same moon, while Amos was rehearsing his stern theme to the herdsmen on the mountain, a pampered son of luxury or a parasitic plebeian in Egypt or Babylon was getting a vicarious sense of validity from stories of the magic lamp or the magic carpet.

The expression "creative vision" may seem a contradiction of terms; yet it is the quality of some men to see that which never has been but which can be within the framework of reality and would add to the quality of living. Such creative vision may become an active cause of events, without which they would not occur. At their best utopians have that gift.

Whatever stirs men deeply tends to result in pictures of a good society. When, a short time before the discovery of America, the Turks overran Greece and drove Greek scholars to Italy, there was a burst of utopian thinking and undertaking in Italian cities. Columbus inspired utopias by opening the doors of what had seemed like a closed world.

When the Tudors broke up the ancient land system of England, other pictures of a good society appeared. The Industrial Revolution, one of the great disturbances of history, stimulated the appearance of utopias at an unprecedented rate. Whenever circumstances press especially hard upon men, unless their spirits are completely broken they persist in picturing a good world that for the present is denied them. When men cease to produce utopias it will be because they are all dead, in spirit, if not in body—or else because life is so good that they cannot imagine it to be better.

√ A sense of human brotherhood, a craving to find some way in which all men, and not just the favored few, could escape from drudgery, has been one of the dominant incentives to the writing of utopias. As Bellamy said, the crux of the problem in his boyhood discussions was "Who would do the dirty work?" To imagine labor-saving technology may have seemed like a psychology of escape; yet that term may sometimes be too easily applied. What seems like wishful thinking may be a refusal to surrender the hope of better things.

This craving to be relieved from the deadening burden of physical drudgery is constantly in evidence in utopian writing and leads to the prophesying of many inventions. Thomas More cautiously felt his way to modern technology, as in forecasting artificial incubation of eggs. First, perhaps, among the moderns to see the freeing of men from drudgery as an important element of the good life was Robert Owen, who spoke and wrote from his knowledge as a successful manufacturer. J. H. Etzler, in one of the first American utopias, *The Paradise Within the Reach of All Men*, published in Pennsylvania in 1833, forecast plastics, synthetic fabrics, and air conditioning. Henry Thoreau read this thin little volume and, repulsed by the crude picture it presented of a mechanized civilization, was confirmed in his preference for simple living. About three years later, in 1836, another Pennsylvanian, Mrs. Mary Griffith, in her little utopia, *Three Hundred Years Hence*, forecast many of the technical developments which have since taken place. In 1840 came Cabet's *Icarie* in which technical inventions were among the most prominent features of a somewhat mechanically organized society.

Then, at about the time of *Looking Backward*, came another burst of utopian writing in which inventions and technical developments were to relieve men of drudgery. Bellamy generally is looked upon as the first to anticipate broadcasting of the human voice, but at least two utopians had preceded him in this: Macnie in *The Diothas*, and Cridge in *Utopia: The History of an Extinct Planet*. Both were published in 1884, the first in New York and the second in California. Macnie also forecast internal combustion engines, wheat "combine harvesters," artificial milk, microphotographs, television, a universal language, and numerous other useful developments. Yet, for all the imaginative daring of utopian writers, the developments of technology in general have already outrun their predictions.

In contrast with most utopians, William Morris was very skeptical of modern technology. In his *News from Nowhere* we have a record of his disgust at the dirty, ugly England of the Industrial Revolution, and his love of his quiet, old-time rural English home where he was reared in simple luxury. Thus typical utopian writings criticize the shortcomings of the prevailing social order as they see them and contrast them to the finest the creator of the utopia has seen or heard about. The sheer creative element generally is small, though the best that the utopian has seen becomes refined and perfected in his own mind, and that process of itself is creative.

As already suggested, there is, in the more responsible utopian literature, a great and largely untapped reservoir of creative ideas and shrewd practical devices, with records of experience, insight, and wisdom. In these writings thoughtful and experienced men have considered what are the principal handicaps to the achievement of personal and social well-being. Sometimes with creative minds, and often with daring originality, they have devised a great variety of ways of meeting social issues. A collection of utopian literature is like a convention of philosophers and statesmen, determined to find ways in which their hard-won philosophies can be put into effect in the actual lives of men.

It would be an important service to mankind, a service which has never yet been rendered, to assemble all such material which is not simply ephemeral or trivial, to organize it into conveniently usable form, and to make it available. One part of such a work would be an analysis and codification of all principles, methods, and devices used in utopias and in near utopias. Under any subject, such as education or money or economic equality or freedom of thought and expression, would be presented the best-thought-out and best-expressed observations, opinions, and policies of utopian writers, with indication of the extent to which different viewpoints prevailed among utopians. From some utopians, such as Plato, More, Rousseau, or Bellamy, a considerable number of significant ideas would be extracted and codified. From the writings of many a minor utopian but a single idea or proposal would be worth recording; yet in the aggregate these scattered contributions would constitute an important part of the whole. Such a "classified compendium of utopian principles and usages," gathered from the entire range of utopian literature, would be an invaluable handbook for lawmakers and all those who formulate public policy.

Not only does utopian literature supply such background material for social design, but the unconventional creative approach of utopians helps us to break through the rigid and formidable barriers of conventional thinking and see things fresh, from unusual standpoints. To some extent utopians provide choice of method, which is the very essence of freedom.

"To write properly the history of utopias from the time of Sir Thomas More to the present is to write the history of the progress of human thought in the past five centuries." Such was the opinion of Charles M. Andrews in his introduction to *Ideal Empires and Republics*. There is reason to believe that the British Royal Society was a direct outgrowth of two or three utopias—Andreae's *Christianopolis*, Bacon's *New Atlantis*, and *Nova Solyma*. Perhaps the most obviously productive of all utopias was Harrington's *Oceana*, which has been discussed. Practical-minded congressmen seldom realize, when they argue for the separation of the legislative, executive, and judicial functions of government, that they are going over the arguments of *Oceana*. Neither are the people of Massachusetts, Pennsylvania, and other states generally aware that their constitutions contain substantial elements borrowed from that source; nor are the French aware of the extent to which the Napoleonic organization of France was, through Sieyès, probably indebted to *Oceana*.

Robert Owen, through his utopian writing and his personal work, gave rise to the great co-operative movement, had a profound effect on education, gave its name and much of its content to socialism, greatly influenced the trade union movement, and was forerunner of the ethical culture movement. The influence of Rousseau's *Social Contract* on government in Europe and America is common knowledge. His influence on education through Pestalozzi, Froebel, Elizabeth Peabody, and Horace Mann is less well known.

The efforts of statesmen to put their plans into practical

effect often are blocked by lack of a great pattern which they can follow. In the aggregate men have a vast amount of energy, but possess small capacity for creative design. They spend their energies in wars, in building economic empire, in ostentation of wealth, because no finer design for living possesses their spirits. Whenever an apparently hopeful design is powerfully presented so as to capture men's attention and loyalty, they will pour vast energies into its realization, even though the design is extremely faulty. Witness the energies which have been poured into efforts to realize the designs presented by Buddha, Mohammed, Rousseau, Karl Marx, Mary Baker Eddy, Joseph Smith of the Mormons, and Adolph Hitler.

No greater service can be done to men than to contribute to the correction, refinement, and enlargement of the designs of life they live by. Efforts to do this by means of pictures of ideal societies, called utopias, rank high among effective means to that end. It is not the immediate application of such a picture to a particular society that is the measure of their greatest usefulness, but the fact that they exist as bases for measuring what has been done and as suggestions of what might be.

Why Utopias Fail

FIRST OF ALL, UTOPIAS FAIL BY DEFINITION. As has been indicated, if a plan of society or of government comes quickly into successful operation, as did the Constitution of the United States, it ceases to be classified as a utopia. Harrington's *Oceana* has almost lost its status as a utopia because it was so widely used in making actual constitutions.

Again, utopias are said to "fail" when they picture an order of society so excellent that its realization will require a very long period. The visions of the Isaiahs are of this character. There is a current saying, "If a man is one step ahead of the crowd he is a leader, if two steps ahead he is a disturber, if three steps he is a fanatic." The great utopias of the world are several or many steps ahead of the crowd. The qualities which make them failures at a particular time may be the very ones that give them enduring value. Elements of Bellamy's utopia which half a century ago made it revolutionary and dangerous, within a few years may be a guide to social stability and conservatism.

Nearly every vagary of which men are capable has found its way into some utopia. To undertake to discuss them would be like trying to describe all the roads that do not lead to where we want to go. In considering why utopias fail, the job is large enough if we confine ourselves to reasons for failure of those proposals which have intrinsic merit.

One of the commonest defects of utopias is the habit of selecting certain elements of a good society and of magnifying them and centering the attention on them to the neglect of other values no less important. One of the most frequent errors of utopians in this respect is overemphasis upon the value of unity, while ignoring those of diversity, freedom, and initiative. The result of such a course at best is a quick achievement of efficiency at the expense of growth in character and culture. Sparta under such a regime maintained military supremacy for centuries, but produced few great men, and its existence would scarcely be remembered but for its relations with individualistic Athens. While Peru achieved great wealth and material development, it was at the expense of other human values.

The analogy of society to a living organism may mislead. We see the unity of co-ordination of all parts of the human body, but we may fail to see that this co-ordination results from diversity instead of from uniformity. The same is true of a mechanism like the automobile. The utopian designer would be mistaken if he should give all his attention to removing friction, for while perfect lubrication and absence of friction is desirable in the bearings, unless the brakes had friction, and unless the tires had friction against the road, the automobile would be useless.

That sense of proportion, with appreciation of all elements of social worth, with wise appraisal of relative values, and with a sense of design, which must be the foundation of a great society, is not a matter of quick discovery or of revolution, but the achievement of gradual growth, creation, design, and discipline. Violence may break down barriers, it may crack the shell when the chick is fully developed, it may be the birth pains of the delivery of a new social order; but it cannot create. The chief value of a great utopia is not primarily in bringing about a sudden revolution, but in contributing new and useful elements which may be incorporated in the process of gradual development. A utopia has not failed so long as it is a productive part of the fabric of men's thoughts.

Another very common reason for the failure of utopias is dilution. The early Christian way of life could not be killed by mass crucifixions, by burnings, by feeding Christians to lions in the arena. But what these terrors could not destroy was undermined by the dilution of spirit which came with multiplication of numbers and with prosperity. Many men and women will join an organization or a movement which promises a better social order. They may have a strong feeling of loyalty. However, as they become economically and socially secure it may develop that what they unconsciously craved was security for the existing pattern of their lives, not a chance to use all their powers to achieve a new pattern. They may begin to talk of personal freedom, meaning freedom to counteract, to dilute, and to destroy the genius of the undertaking they were so eager to join.

How can this type of failure be prevented? Sometimes by careful selection of participants, whether by personal choice of members of a small fellowship, or wise sifting of national immigration; sometimes by a period of probation and training, as in preparation for citizenship; nearly always with complete freedom of criticism and inquiry, so that warps and limitations of the undertaking may become evident; by the constant striving for universality of outlook, combined with intense commitment to the ideal of the undertaking; and lastly by the elimination of those who are fundamentally out of harmony with the spirit and aims of the project, as is brought about when criminals are removed from a free society.

Another chief cause of the failure of utopias is neglect of the process of educating and conditioning the minds and spirits of men to harmonize with the utopian aims. To Anacharsis, the great Scythian from the plains north of the Black Sea, who lived two centuries before Plato, is attributed a searching discussion of this need, a statement in which he looked still further back to the principles of legislation adopted by Lycurgus at Sparta:

"Nature is almost always in opposition to the laws; because she labours for the happiness of the individual, without regard to the other individuals who surround him: while the laws only direct their attention to the relations by which he is united to them; and because nature infinitely diversifies our character and inclinations, while it is the object of the laws to bring them back to unity. The legislator, therefore, whose aim it is to annihilate, or at least to reconcile these contrarities, must consider morals as the most powerful spring, and most essential part, of his political institutions. He must take the work of nature almost at the first moment she has produced it, retouch its form and proportions, and soften without entirely effacing its great outlines; till at length he has converted the independent man into the free citizen."

"All who have meditated on the art of governing mankind, have been convinced that the fate of empires depended on the education given to youth; and from their reflections we may lay it down as an evident principle, that education, the laws, and manners, ought never to contradict each other." [1]

Were Anacharsis writing today, doubtless he would include with "nature" the indoctrinated commonplace cultural tradition which holds blindly to the patterns of the past. In the fanciful little English utopia of more than a century ago, *The Revolt of the Bees*, in which this quotation from Anacharsis occurs, there is a formula for overcoming such discrepancy between the prevailing bent of life and the requirements for the realization of utopia:

.... those means employed with such extraordinary success by Lycurgus in generating the martial character, we have applied with equal success, and with the certainty of more lasting effect, in producing the intelligent and benevolent. Those means are comprehended in the following principles:

1st, An unremitting attention to the early association of ideas.

2nd, The formation of good habits.

3rd, In all our regulations preserving a conformity between the duties of individuals and their most pleasurable and early imbibed ideas,—thus uniting the agreeable with the useful.[2]

We may safely and profitably follow this advice if we are careful always to maintain freedom of inquiry and of communication, so that errors or lack of great quality in the pattern of utopia may be brought to light and remedied.

Another cause of the failures of utopias is the common belief that, once started properly on their way, they will be self-operating, self-purifying, and self-continuing. This mistaken view was expressed in a utopia of a century ago, *The Peopling of Utopia*, by Samual Bower: "Every true votary of freedom believes that the popular principle once having gained a preponderance in the legislature, would be able to surround itself with all the conditions of durability; and that, whatever the form of government through which it might operate, justice would be constantly its object, and the fullest measure of justice its final result. . . ." [3]

The history of human institutions has provided frequent refutations of this theory, yet it has been the practical working philosophy of many a utopian effort. Its mention leads to the consideration of another cause of the failure of utopia which, notwithstanding its importance in all ages and in every land, has not been adequately appraised. This ancient and ubiquitous cause of failure is the "racket."

Perhaps no other reason for failure of good social order is so universal. It is natural for honest men of good will to give their attention to their own work, and to expect others to do likewise. This attitude tends to leave them disarmed and subject to exploitation. In a community of a thousand persons nine hundred and fifty may thus be going about their business sincerely; yet if the other fifty make it their primary business, not to produce wealth, but to manipulate affairs so as to appropriate wealth or power for themselves, very often they can succeed.

When the strategy of getting power is their chief interest and exercise, men may become highly skilled in it, as the great majority are not. The power seekers can study the public mind, its weaknesses and foibles. They can plot their way into strategic positions. They can make friendships and alignments; and before the great majority that is going quietly about its business is aware, it may be in the grip of this power-planning group, with "worth on foot, and rascals in the coach."

This institution of the racket is very old, and its technique is well developed. Along the mountain highways of eastern Europe at every strategic point one comes upon the ruins of a castle, where in days gone by some robber baron lived and levied tax on every caravan of traders that passed by. His descendant, through the control of banks or other agencies of business, may be no less well situated to take tribute from all who pass.

In America recently it was reported that every artichoke which went from a California garden and every egg from a Utah farm to a New York market paid its tribute to a racketeer. It is reported that every pound of mica which is mined must, on its way to market, pay tribute to a small control group. In a hundred or a thousand industries, large and small, the process is repeated. In most cities, towns, villages, and counties, while the average decent citizens who make up most of the population go about their business, a little group of men, laying their lines and planning deliberately, have taken possession of the local government. One of our stronger labor unions did not have a convention or an election for ten years. The president found a way to get control, and laid aside a fortune while in that position. Some other unions have had a not greatly different career. In various American industries, notwithstanding antitrust litigation, the control of the industry by a small inner ring is almost complete. Some of the most persistent and oppressive rackets men have known have been in the name of religion.

Underlying the ancient and widespread institution of the racket is the fundamental fact that usually men become skillful and accomplished only at the occupation to which they give their time, their attention, and their interest. People who are intent on producing and on serving become skillful primarily in such activity, and are at a disadvantage in the control of affairs as compared with those who are intent on organizing situations and seizing power. Men are so adaptable that in a large and complex society, given almost any conceivable form of social organization, the racketeer can study and master the operations of that social order and can make it serve his purpose. It is doubtful, therefore, whether the racket ever can be permanently eliminated from society merely by a form of social and economic organization, though some forms serve its purpose much better than others.

What then is our hope? Partly that so long as racketeers are active, men shall divide their attention between production and vigilance, as the pioneer used to carry along a cumbersome gun while following the plow; partly that intelligence and good will shall be better organized; and partly that education and the dissemination of intelligence shall make men less credulous. Above all, perhaps, ultimate relief from the racket will come from widespread refinement and strengthening of character. Men of social purpose will not envy or admire racketeers, nor invest in their projects for the sake of the dividends. With growth of character they will come to have an intuitive, accurate appraisal of motives. Men of courage will not be watching to see which will be the winning side in any alignment, so that they may join it, but will persistently align themselves with men whose motives and methods they can respect regardless of immediate prospects for success or failure. Cowardice and desire to share in the perquisites of rackets are among the most potent causes of their continuance.

Utopias would more often succeed if men more generally had that capacity for foresight and sustained interest which would lead them wisely to define long-range plans and to persist in working for their realization. The old Chinese in drilling for petroleum set a good example for utopians. According to accounts of engineers who have studied Chinese drilling methods, to drive an oil well two thousand feet deep with the primitive drilling equipment then available would require about three generations. Year after year through a man's lifetime, and the lifetimes of his son and his grandson, the slow drilling would proceed; while the family lived in poverty, with great exercise of thrift and self-restraint. When finally the oil sands were reached, generations of economic well-being were assured.

For long-range undertakings the prospects of success must be very carefully weighed before the long effort is begun. And so with the pursuit of utopias. The elemental drives of men are attuned to short periods of effort. Under primitive conditions of life, where the chance and caprice of circumstance largely rule, an aim which cannot be quickly realized had better be abandoned in favor of other pursuits, the difficulty of which may happily be less. In view of the superficial and casual life aims of many men in which the goals may be either trivial or inherently out of reach, weakness of will in pursuing those aims may be a protection against continued waste of effort. Persistence and wisdom should develop together.

With the conditions of complex civilization, and with increased definition of long-time aims, the achievement of great social objectives requires longer periods, and the capacity of the average man for sustained interest and commitment commonly is not equal to such undertakings. There is doubt as to whether the Christian church would have survived the first years but for a vivid expectation of the almost immediate coming of the Kingdom of Heaven. As has been said before, had Bellamy timed his utopia for the year 6000 instead of having it an old story by A.D. 2000, it might have fallen flat. The prospect of so long an effort would have exceeded the general capacity for sustained interest and purpose.

To a superficial observer it may seem that utopian writings have influence only on those who lack a sense of humor, and that the least suggestion by a utopian or a philosopher that he is not fully convinced of his own ideas will sound the death-knell of his prestige. Of those few utopians or philosophers who have survived after causing people to smile, nearly all have been popularly consigned to the status of entertainers, as witness Jonathan Swift's *Gulliver's Travels* and Hans Christian Andersen's *Fairy Tales*, which too seldom are read beyond the school years. One of the few cases of success in ignoring this precept of solemnity by a utopian or a philosopher is that of Lewis Carroll. It appears that some utopians and philosophers prefer Alice's Wonderland to their own.

An example of the danger of levity is that charming and penetrating utopia by Don Marquis, *The Almost Perfect State*. Don Marquis smiled at himself and his ideas, and with what result? No reference to his utopia has been found by the writer in any comprehensive treatment of the subject. It is not even listed under philosophy or utopias in the library, but under humor!

Who knows what wise utopians or philosophers, almost ready to lead the people to a new age, have lost that opportunity and have sunk to oblivion, because they were so rash as to smile at themselves and their ideas, and to admit doubt of their own infallibility?

Perhaps, however, the public makes a very subtle distinction. It may come to love a philosopher who smiles *with* himself and his ideas, as did Lewis Carroll, but it will be no more than casually entertained by one who smiles *at* himself and his ideas, especially if there is a suspicion that he smiles because he has not the courage to stand by his ideas and desires to be in a position to disown them.

Only rarely does a utopian writer have both the insight and the honesty with himself to tell why his utopia fails, as did Don Marquis. At the end of his utopia he wrote:

... the Almost Perfect State must be previsioned, planned, brought into existence and maintained by a succession of prophets.

Prophets who can ride herd and direct when the "instincts" of the cattle set them moving. . . . Prophets who shall reveal Sinai and Olympus and lead and prod their people up the difficult ascents.

The whole thing is as simple as that!

Whenever I am tempted to go into detail as to just how to get these Prophets, I pause before I write—pause, and fill a pipe, and reflect. And as I reflect, a certain mocking devil always at my elbow lights the pipe. And the world, which was just about to be saved, swings cheerily onward once more in the orbit of iniquity.

And so in the end the articles dribble away—and the book fails . . . precisely because the writer does not know how to get these Prophets who are to bring into being the Almost Perfect State. . . . The author does not know how to get Prophets, primarily, because he does not know how to be one himself. But the failure derives from a deeper source even than that—*it is evident that the author did not steadily desire to be one.*

...it is also somewhat melancholy to realize now the chance I had in the theme and see how grievously I fumbled it in the execution. [The book was assembled from a newspaper column.] On the one hand, I am not so hot after an Almost Perfect State as I was then; and on the other hand, I am less patient with my own auto-irony and self-mockery. I had something here by the tail, if I had only possessed the courage and industry to take it a little more seriously. But while I was exclaiming over how funny the quirks in the tail were, the thing itself got away from me. There is scarcely a page that does not recall to the writer himself some phase of a long struggle within himself, that culminated certainly in no definite victory either for his gaiety or his sincerity. But all this makes no difference to anybody else.[4]

Among many causes of the failure of utopias is this—that few utopians who were convincing as to their full sanity have fully trusted their own visions. Socrates was old when he drank the hemlock, and Plato seems not greatly to have sacrificed himself over his *Republic*. Thomas More apologized for his utopia within its very pages, so much so that those who prepared the "build-up" for his canonization could claim that he did not believe in major portions of it himself. It was perhaps less burdensome for the blessed St. Thomas More to get his elderly head cut off than it would have been for him to live by the utopia he visioned in his young manhood. Francis Bacon never suffered for his *Atlantis*. William Dean Howells, we are told, soon turned away from such works as *A Traveller from Altruria* to a more lucrative field. Macnie apparently was long apologetic for *The Diothas*.

There is another breed of utopians for whom men have a different feeling. The young man, Jesus, on the cross; Robert Owen, spending his all for his dream; Edward Bellamy, giving his life for his vision—these move us more deeply. Even Hitler, with his crude, brutal, backward-looking utopia, by throwing himself so completely into it, made the world shake.

We may laugh *with* our dreams, but not *at* them.

When we examine some of the causes of the failure of utopias, we must reach the conclusion that many of these causes run deep in the cultural patterns of mankind. No legislative change, no revolution in the form of society, will take away the necessity for the long, slow growth which must prepare men for a new Golden Age. Yet, as wax is rigid when cold, pliable when warm, and flows freely when hot, so, though the spirits and habits of men may seem rigid and frozen, they may become ductile or even liquid, and may take on new forms with surprising rapidity, if they are warmed by a great personality, by great trials, or by great events. Then it is fortunate if a great pattern has been envisioned and is ready for them.

IX

Beyond Utopia

A map of the world that does not include Utopia is not worth even glancing at, for it leaves out the one country at which Humanity is always landing. And when Humanity lands there, it looks out, and, seeing a better country, sets sail. Progress is the realization of Utopias.—Oscar Wilde, *The Soul of Man under Socialism.*[1]

IT IS INHERENT IN HUMAN NATURE TO tend to give greatest attention and greatest weight to the most immediate needs and desires. A boy or girl longs to finish grade school and to leave childhood and its inferior status behind. That step seems to be the greatest of a lifetime. A few years later, as higher schooling draws to a close, there is intense desire to be "on one's own," and again that one step seems so important that, in comparison with it, the remaining problems of life appear to be simple. Then follows desire for a mate and for a home, and so it continues through life; at each point the next step appears to be the one important remaining hurdle.

There are some universal cravings which, being seldom fully satisfied, accumulate in the general social consciousness until their satisfaction seems to be *the* great human need. Men think that if these wants should be filled, the remaining way would be clear. Whoever concentrates his attention on them is thought to be a "practical" person; whoever shows keen interest in more distant ends is frequently classed as idealist or dreamer.

Utopias for the most part have dealt with elemental needs of men, such as abundance of food, shelter, and clothing; freedom from oppression, freedom from excessive toil; peace and leisure, and opportunity for self-expression free from frustration. To present a clear picture of a society in which these needs would be securely met is to make a moving appeal to the spirits of men. There is a general conviction that, given fulfillment of human need in these respects, life would be good, and that if any problems should remain they would be of less critical import and could be faced with confidence.

This conviction survives the nearly universal experience of everyday life that as any goal is won, no matter how eagerly it has been sought, the satisfaction of its possession tends to fade, and other cravings arise in its place. This almost universal expectation, though contrary to almost universal human experience, is evidence of the importance which immediate incentives play in biological survival.

So rarely is it the lot of men to fulfill all their obvious needs and desires that seldom are they without immediate pressing wants, and seldom does the question arise as to what would be the value of living if all these needs should be securely filled. Edward Bellamy, in one of his notebooks, pointed out one advantage of the pursuit of wealth. He wrote, "The fact that all the world goes after money saves a man the necessity of anxiously debating what his life is for." [2] Even to raise the question implies an impractical vein in the questioner. Yet a discussion of utopia which does not look beyond utopia is sadly incomplete. It may even be true that until one has looked beyond utopia, and thereby has seen it in its larger setting, his view of utopia will be so out of perspective as to be misleading.

Beyond Utopia 179

What lies beyond utopia? The answer differs greatly for different people. There are men of so coarse texture that only animal satisfactions appeal to them. Take away interest in food and sex and in the excitement of physical activity, such as sports or war, and their life becomes flat. Other men and women are somewhat more highly organized, and find the stimulus of ambition to be less evanescent. Such persons supply much of the leadership in business, in politics, and in social competition.

All primitive incentives are highly subject to fading. As we ascend the scale of human interests, increasingly we find values that are more enduring. But even this is not a universal rule. Whoever wrote Ecclesiastes gave the world's classic expression to the disillusionment which so generally accompanies the fulfillment of specific human hopes:

I communed with mine own heart, saying, Lo, I am come to great estate, and have gotten more wisdom than all they that have been before me in Jerusalem; yea, my heart had great experience of wisdom and knowledge. And I gave my heart to know wisdom, and to know madness and folly: I perceived that this also is vexation of spirit.[3]

I said in mine heart, Go to now, I will prove thee with mirth, therefore enjoy pleasure; and, behold, this also is vanity. I made me great works; I builded me houses; I planted me vineyards; I made me gardens and orchards ... And whatsoever mine eyes desired I kept not from them, I withheld not my heart from any joy ... Then I looked on all the works that my hands had wrought ... and, behold, all was vanity and vexation of spirit ... Therefore I hated life ...[4]

Madame de Maintenon, beautiful, intelligent, and influential wife of Louis XIV, re-echoed the words of this preacher of ancient times: "I have been young and beautiful," she wrote to her niece, "I have tasted many pleasures; I have been universally beloved. At a more advanced age

I have passed years in the intercourse of talent and wit, and I solemnly protest to you, that all conditions leave a frightful void."

The writer recalls the pathetic, eager seriousness with which a man of great wealth once asked him to bear his message to the students of Antioch College. "Won't you tell them," he said, "that riches do not bring happiness?" Since but few can achieve material wealth, and not all of them have a feeling of social responsibility and capacity for expressing reflective thought, there are not many who will send such a message, and perhaps even fewer who will believe it. The chorus in *Oedipus* has echoed numberless times in the souls of men who were baffled by satiety or by seemingly inexorable fate:

> Nothingness, nothingness
> Ye Children of Man, and less
>   I count you, waking or dreaming!
> And none among mortals, none,
> Seeking to live, hath won
> More than to seem, and to cease
>   Again from his seeming.[5]

A man's body can live in but a very narrow range of temperature. A little too hot or too cold, and he suffers; with greater extremes, he dies. Similarly a man can thrive in but a narrow range as to wants; that is, if needs are too pressing, life ceases, or loses its zest. When all his wants are filled, he may perish of tedium. Between the pressure of too much want, which kills the spirits of men, and makes them wish they never had been born; and the satiating of all desire, which leaves life flat and tasteless, or even repulsive, man must steer his course with wisdom, with humility and self-control, and perchance with faith. The zest which we would have for life must be maintained by travail of spirit. It will not of necessity follow any material utopia.

Edward Bellamy once hinted at the problem when he quoted:

> ". . . he who would be barred capacity
> Of pain, courts incapacity of bliss." [6]

Inequality of wealth—it is an ill wind that does no good—has had some beneficial effects. Not the least of these is in revealing to us that utopia may not mean felicity. Were all men equally poor and in need, they might all alike believe that material abundance would surely bring happiness (as so large a part of mankind believes now), and there would be no one to point out their delusion. Then, when abundance should be secured for all, what universal disillusionment would result! Perhaps mankind could not survive such unanimous disappointment. Is it not fortunate that some men, favored with all that wealth and position can buy, have served as scouts—to spy out the land and bring back reports of what they found?

Such men tell us that happiness is far more complex and elusive than we have realized. Few will believe them, yet those who believe least very often have no resources of interest except animal appetites. As Moses led his people forty years in the wilderness, until they should have the stamina to live in the Promised Land, do not men today need training for abundance before it is thrown into their laps? Is it not of the highest importance that we prepare for utopia by thinking beyond it?

Utopia will not answer the more profound problems of life. It will only release men from immediate preoccupation with material want so that they can be aware of deeper issues. For every hundred men who can stand adversity, there may be only ten, or only one, who can stand utopia. Shakespeare has Hecate say in *Macbeth:*

> And you all know security
> Is mortals' chiefest enemy.

Terrible as world conditions are, the great problem of mankind today is not to achieve utopia, but to be prepared to survive it. A beautiful world is further away than a well-fed prosperous one. John Buchan wrote: "It was not the return of the dark ages that I feared, but the coming of a too garish age, when life would be lived in the glare of neon lamps and the Spirit would have no solitude."

What would men do in utopia? They would do the things they had learned along the way; only for those things would they have appetites, only in them would they take pleasure. What would Alexander the Great do in utopia? He would start out to conquer the world, not because of poverty or hunger, not because of "the economic determination of history," but because of a dominant physiological drive, or because his spirit would crave expression to escape boredom, and he would know no other way. It was Alexander's great tutor and teacher, Aristotle, who said in his *Politics:*

> There are crimes of which the motive is want; and for these Phaleas expects to find a cure in the equalization of property, which will take away from a man the temptation to be a highwayman, because he is hungry and cold. But want is not the sole incentive to crime; men desire to gratify some passion which preys upon them, or they are eager to enjoy the pleasures which are unaccompanied with pain, and therefore they commit crimes. .... The fact is that the greatest crimes are caused by excess and not by necessity. Men do not become tyrants in order that they may not suffer cold...the institutions of Phaleas avail only against petty crimes.

Edward Bellamy, keen observer that he was, writing in his journal at the age of twenty-two, expressed about the same opinion as Aristotle:

It is probably erroneous to suppose that the desire of transmitting wealth to descendants or leaving it to our families is a motive essential to great zeal in the accumulation of riches. . . . If very rich men are childless as they often are, or wifeless as they are likely to be, do we observe them less devoted to their passion of accumulation? . . . the gold-hunters prosecute their endless task because, by the subtle process of association of ideas, wealth in itself has come to seem valuable to them, although the only ends for which it is valuable are long ago secured. . . . For all that appears then men would continue to accumulate wealth with the same avidity although the right of inheritance were cut off and their wealth went, as in fact it does generally go, and as they foresee well enough it will go, to the four winds of heaven.[7]

It is not only among men of power that interests are determined by the cultural set of mind, rather than by opportunity. I recall as a boy hearing the talk of two farmer boys who had returned from the Chicago World's Fair of 1893. Though within reach of all its marvels, their days had alternated between the Chicago stock yards and houses of prostitution. They would have the same interests in utopia, and whether or not satisfaction of those interests was provided, they soon would find life unutterably dull.

If all men were today transported to utopia, for a time they would be on vacation. They would rest their weary bones, and would eat what they always had desired but hitherto could not afford. Then boredom would begin. They would seek stirring experience. Limited to the range of interests they had achieved, they would do those things for which they had appetite and interests. To a large degree they would do things which, by their very nature, would destroy utopia. Elements of utopia have been achieved many times in human societies, only to be marred or destroyed because men's culture was not equal to their opportunities.

Economic and social justice may maintain a controlled

range of economic temperature within which life may function best, but it will not supply lasting incentives for living, nor will it find them already in existence. They must be achieved. In the end we are driven back to that age-old truth, "The kingdom of heaven is within you." It is well that the approach to utopia be gradual, so that little by little we may be tempered to the unprecedented demands it will put upon the human spirit.

But just as in physical life, too hot or too cold are equally fatal, so too much want is as destructive as too little. Society still has far to go to achieve that degree of economic well-being in which, while man must work to live, life for many is not so difficult as to discourage a search for enduring values. It is well for the approach to utopia to be uninterrupted, for time not spent in motion is time lost, and it may be death.

Given a state of society in which there is neither satiety nor extreme want, if the energies and interests of men should come to be focused on achievements of imperishable worth, instead of being consumed in conflict with each other or with external nature, each decade might see as great progress toward the goal as does a century today. The way at best will be long and difficult, yet it is faith that the potential values of life are worth living and working for which gives courage, hope, and enthusiasm to thinking men.

APPENDIX

NOTES

INDEX

APPENDIX

CONCERNING VOYAGES TO SOUTH AMERICA BEFORE AND
SHORTLY AFTER COLUMBUS, AND TRIPS FROM THE AT-
LANTIC COAST TO PERU BEFORE PIZARRO

Since for four hundred years it has been assumed that
More could not have received information about Peru, in-
asmuch as he wrote *Utopia* about twelve years before Pizarro discovered the country, it seems desirable to present
more abundant and varied evidence than otherwise would
be necessary to show that More might well have had information directly from Peru, very much, if not exactly,
in the manner he describes in the introduction to his account
of Utopia.

So far as we can discover, information relating to the possibility of More's acquaintance with Peru has never been
assembled. Both because of its pertinence to this subject,
and also in order that the references found may be readily
available, an extended account of the source material is presented here. This evidence is presented under the following
heads:

1. For decades before and after Columbus' voyages, as
a matter of self-protection, Portugal had a vigorous policy
of secrecy concerning her discoveries, and went to the length
of systematically suppressing and destroying records. There
is much evidence that numerous voyages were made of
which no record exists beyond brief incidental references.

2. Almost certainly there were several, perhaps a considerable number, of Portuguese voyages to the east coast
of South America, the time of which would have allowed

information to reach Thomas More before he wrote *Utopia*.

3. The Indians along the east coast of South America knew of the fabulous kingdom of Peru, had well-traveled trade routes thither, and brought back gold, silver, and copper articles, some of which were taken to Europe by explorers. At least some, and probably most, of the voyagers to the east coast of South America learned of the Inca Empire.

4. There are definite records of at least three expeditions to the land of the Incas, made by Europeans from the south Atlantic coast, before Pizarro reached it from the Pacific. These expeditions took about the same route as that described in More's *Utopia*.

Let us first consider the policy of secrecy.

The assumption so frequently and aggressively expressed, that since we have no records of other early voyages to South America, no others were made, is not justified. A. E. Nordenskiöld, in his *Facsimile Atlas*, wrote:

It is generally supposed that the successful voyages of the Portuguese ... and the re-discovery of the New World by Columbus must have made a great and immediate impression throughout Christendom. ... Yet, this was so far from being the case, that scarcely any discovery of importance was received with so much indifference.[1]

Then, describing the thorough search by Mr. Henry Harrisse for documents of that period, he continued:

Scarcely one work containing an original communication about the New World of the length of at least one printed page, was annually published during the first fifty years after the discovery of Columbus, and all these original communications together would be easily comprised in a single volume of very moderate size. ...

Still poorer is the oldest printed literature of maps. ... I speak

of printed, not of manuscript maps. Tolerably complete map-
sketches drawn to illustrate the reports of explorers or adventurers
were probably made for the government or the ship-owners after
almost every more or less successful voyage, but they were seldom
published. They generally seem to have been jealously concealed
in public or private archives. Most of them have since been lost, or
exhumed from the dust of libraries for the first time in the present
century.[2]

The reason for suppression of information by the Portuguese is frequently referred to by students of early exploration. At that time Portugal was the weakest of the maritime
powers, with a population of only 1,500,000. Spain, Venice,
and Florence, her great rivals, were far stronger in men,
wealth, and vessels, though Portugal had able and daring
seamen. Under these circumstances Portugal endeavored by
secrecy to hold her own.

Charles E. Nowell, in his article, "The Discovery of Brazil
—Accidental or Intentional?" writes of Portuguese knowledge of America, "Portugal knew always far more than was
revealed." [3]

Percy Alvin Martin, writing in the *Hispanic American
Historical Review*, emphasized the same condition: "This
policy of secrecy, necessary perhaps to a small country like
Portugal, has proven one of the greatest obstacles to a full
investigation of the period." [4]

In his "Supposed Discovery of South America before
1448," J. Batalha-Reis gives numerous cases and considerable evidence to indicate that Portuguese historians, as records are now known, failed to report many voyages, including important ones, taken during the fourteenth and fifteenth
centuries. In various instances, knowledge of a voyage or a
voyager depends on a single reference, some of these being
discovered only in recent years. In some cases original manu-
scripts are lost, and we know of them only by reference in

other writings. For instance, Batalha-Reis states: "No Portuguese historian refers to the expeditions sent by [King] D. Affonso IV. of Portugal (from before 1336 to 1341), to make discoveries on the Atlantic." [5] Again he states that Ruy de Pina, official chronicler of Brazil, discussing the supposed discovery of America before 1448, wrote, "King D. Affonso's memoirs . . . by neglect or want of writers, were not less forgotten or wasted than his (the king's) flesh and body, which the earth is eating up." [6] Batalha-Reis further quotes old Portuguese historians as stating that no list has been found of the armadas of vessels which sailed from Lisbon to discover the seacoasts of Africa and Asia, nor in the Atlantic.

William Brooks Greenlee wrote in 1937 for the Hakluyt Society on "The Voyage of Pedro Alvares Cabral to Brazil and India":

Unfortunately few records of the early navigations now remain. This was partly due to the neglect in their preservation in the Torre do Tombo . . . but chiefly because of a policy of secrecy which it was felt necessary to maintain. Not only have almost all the early records disappeared but also many of the chronicles [official historical records]. Even the writings of the historians of the sixteenth century were under such strict supervision that they cannot always be trusted.[7]

Finally, Edgar Prestage, foremost English authority on Portuguese history, in his "Search for the Sea Route to India" wrote:

[Under Afonso V of Portugal, who reigned 1460-1481] a policy of secrecy was adopted, which included the suppression of information that might serve competitors. . . . Even in Henry's lifetime [he died in 1460] Afonso V had a Castilian in his service who acted as "reader of the Chronicles and books of Castile."

The strange silence preserved by Portuguese Chronicles of the fifteenth century about the discoveries is thus explicable. When

Barros [8] came to write of them, he could find no complete copy of Zurara's *Chronicle of Guinea,* and he declares that more discoveries were made in the reign of Afonso V than those he relates.

Pina composed in the sixteenth century the Chronicles of the Kings of the preceding century, using the works of his predecessors, but he omitted to speak of the most important event and chief glory of the age, the voyages and discoveries. Nothing but the official policy of secrecy can account for his silence; as royal Chronicler he must have acted under orders, for otherwise he would not have dared to leave out notable achievements in the recording of which many persons then living had an interest. The disappearance of the earlier and more complete books can only be attributed to the policy of secrecy; they were almost certainly destroyed.

The policy of secrecy not only led to the suppression of historical works;—nautical guides, maps, instructions to navigators and their reports suffered the same fate.[9]

Prestage concludes: "We have hardly any information about the Atlantic voyages to the West in the last half of the fifteenth century, though we know that some were made." [10]

This silence was not due to ignorance or carelessness. Prestage, in the article on "Portuguese Literature" in the *Encyclopaedia Britannica* (Fourteenth Edition), of which he is joint author, states concerning the fifteenth century in Portugal:

....the fifteenth century.... is noted for its chronicles.... Fernao Lopez, the father of Portuguese history and author of Chronicles of King Pedro, King Ferdinand, and King John I, has been called by Southey the best Chronicler of any age or nation.

Speaking of Lopez and of the other great Chroniclers, Azurara and de Pina, Prestage adds, "All these three writers combined the posts of keeper of the archives and royal Chronicler, and were, in fact, the King's men." Absence of records is the result of deliberate policy.

In spite of this policy of secrecy, many stories must have leaked out, for Lisbon harbor was a busy place during that period. Prestage wrote in his "Search for the Sea Route to India":

> According to the historian Fernam Lopes, as many as 400 or 500 merchant ships often lay before the city [Lisbon] at one time, while 100 or 150 loaded salt and wine at Sacavem and Montijo in the outskirts. Many of these vessels, if not most, belonged to foreigners.[11]

We shall not tire the reader with more evidence of the policy of secrecy and its effect on public records. Emphasis on this point is necessary, since, when we come to consider the earliest voyages to America, we find ourselves not so much in an atmosphere of dispassionate historical inquiry as in a heated partisan controversy, with frequent assumption that since records of voyages are not at hand, no voyages were made. This partisan tendency is referred to by Batalha-Reis in his "Supposed Discovery of South America before 1448":

> Almost all the historians of geographical discoveries consider it their absolute duty to arrive at a radical conclusion in the study of problematical questions, answering with a *yes* what only deserves a *perhaps*, or, more frequently, dismissing with a *no* what ought to be held as probable.[12]

References to this partisan spirit, especially in the controversy over the relative merits of Vespucci and Columbus, are frequent.

Next, let us consider the evidence that the fame of Peru had spread to the Atlantic coast and was known to the Indians there at the time of the first visits of white men.

The Guarani Indians, who inhabited the eastern part of South America for a distance of three thousand miles or more, were great travelers and traders. When domestic fowls were brought from Europe they were soon distributed all over South America, from the Atlantic to the Pacific. Nordenskiöld and others have presented much evidence of such rapid cultural diffusion.

Greenlee, writing for the Hakluyt Society in 1937, stated that the Indians of Brazil, as found by Cabral on his voyage in 1500, had gold and silver which they got from the Andes. He adds:

The comparative rapidity of these movements is shown by the distribution of those introduced by the Europeans. Between the first relations of these peoples with those of Europe soon after Cabral's voyage and the conquest of Peru by Pizarro, the two elements which spread most rapidly were chickens and iron fishhooks.[13]

Erland Nordenskiöld, one of the most thorough students of early South America, wrote in his *Ethnographic Studies:*

Ramirez states explicitly that the Indians from the Rio Parana went to the mountains in the west, where they fetched metal. The vast extent of the Andes was known in [Sebastian] Cabot's time [1525] to the Indians on the Rio Parana. [He brought back silver ornaments which had been acquired by Indians in trade with Peru.[14]] They even knew there was another ocean behind the mountains.

The fame of the Inca Empire had led to Aleja Garcia's plundering expedition from the Brazilian coast through Chaco to Charcas [Inca country] as early as 1521 [six years before Pizarro's first trip to Peru]. . . .

As a brisk trade was undoubtedly carried on between the Indians of the Andes and the Guarani Indians on the Rio Parana and in southern Brazil, it is not improbable that a European cultural element may have reached these parts from the east long before the conquest of the Inca Empire by Pizarro. . . . Gold, silver, and copper reached the Guarani Indians by barter from the Inca Empire, and these Indians, as we have seen, had quantities of fowls a good many years before the conquest of the Inca Empire. . . .

It was evidently by trade among the Indian tribes . . . that fowls spread so rapidly over vast stretches of the country from one tribe to another.[15]

In another of his works Erland Nordenskiöld reaches the conclusion that "This trade [with the Incas by Paraguay Indians] was, of course, not new in 1526, but it must have flourished in pre-Columbian times. It is quite feasible that in this way metal objects from the Inca country found their way to the coast of Brazil."[16] According to Nordenskiöld, knowledge of the Inca wealth and civilization was very general in the Argentine region. In another of his studies he states that European fowls were introduced into the Inca empire by trade with the Atlantic coast Indians long before Pizarro's conquest. In fact, the last Inca was named after the fowl.[17]

Nordenskiöld further states that "On the R. Ucayali the Indians had evidently not only heard reports about the Inca Empire; *there were also Indians who had been there.*" Hohermuth von Speier, in 1536, in traveling along the headwaters of the Orinoco, crossed the Apure and Casanare rivers, and hence southwest, hearing everywhere about the riches beyond the mountains. They knew the llama by the same name as used by the Incas. "All these accounts about the Inca Empire which the first conquerors heard far away from the actual district of that dominion show how far its fame had spread."[18]

Philip Ainsworth Means, after years of study and research, summed up his conclusion on the matter as follows:

In short, the fame of the Inca Empire . . . spread all the way to the Atlantic Ocean by following the downward course of the

Amazon in the north and of the Paraguay-LaPlata in the south.
... The rumors of Incaic greatness first reached the Atlantic at
the mouths of the Amazon and of the LaPlata, but later it spread
along the Brazilian coast between the two.[19]

He gives a long list of references in support of his conclusion.

Now let us consider evidences of voyages to South
America either before Columbus or early enough thereafter to have made it possible for news to have reached
Thomas More before he wrote *Utopia.* There is, in fact,
considerable evidence that South America and, to a lesser
degree, the West Indies, were known to Portuguese explorers and to natives of north Africa before and after
Columbus' first voyage, and before More wrote *Utopia.*
Several writers, among them J. Batalha-Reis, previously
quoted, describe the nautical map of 1448 by Andrea Bianco.
On this map, near the Cape Verde Islands off the western-
most extension of Africa, is the expression, "Authentic island
is distant 1500 miles to the west." Near the west edge of
the map a sketch of this "authentic" coastline is shown. It
has in general the shape of the easternmost extension of
South America over a distance of between 500 and 1000
miles. After a lengthy discussion Batalha-Reis concludes that
in 1448 Andrea Bianco (Venetian map maker) believed that
somebody had certainly seen an island, that this island was,
at least, more than 500 miles from west to east (only the
easterly coast of the "island" is sketched on the map), that
the island was southwest of Cape Verde, and at a great distance from it (the actual distance from Brazil to Cape Verde
is 1520 miles).

Batalha-Reis continues his description:

Precisely of the year 1447, to which Mr. Yule Oldham more
especially attributes the discovery of the *Authentic Island,* Faria e

Sousa writes… "Other *armadas* were sent by *Infante* D. Henrique, *of which neither the number nor the epic are known.*" [20]

There have been various questions raised concerning the legend on this old map, as, for instance, whether the indistinct last zero of the faded figure "1500" might be an ink blot.

After mentioning the discoveries and armadas of 1469, Faria e Sousa continues, "Previous to this there were other discoveries, of which the authors are unknown . . . and others which have been forgotten."

Las Casas, who with his father was on one voyage with Columbus, who spent most of his life in the New World, and whose writings are a major source of information concerning the period, is given by Batalha-Reis as authority for the statement: "Before 1460, one ship seems to have reached an unknown land, no doubt to the west, and possibly to the south-west, where the navigators, fearing the natives, did not remain a long time, coming back to Portugal with news to the *Infante* D. Henrique." [21] Also, Batalha-Reis states, "Between 1474 and 1496, João Coelho sails to the south-west, and is supposed to have found desert lands, where he died with all his companions, with the exception of two who managed to come back." [22] Reis lists between 15 and 20 projects and expeditions headed westward between 1436 and 1500.

Even Columbus' own first voyage seems to be evidence of earlier discoveries. We are reminded by Percy Alvin Martin:

> Columbus married the daughter of Bartholomew Perestrello, the captain-donatory of Porto Santo of the Madeira group, one of the outposts of the Portuguese in the Atlantic. His mother-in-law placed her husband's charts and papers at his disposal and if we are to believe Ferdinand Columbus [son of the discoverer] and Las Casas [his contemporary biographer] he was convinced by

the study of these documents that lands existed in the western ocean and that it was possible to find them.[23]

After Columbus' first voyage a papal bull was issued in 1493 dividing the western world between Spain and Portugal. It gave to Portugal the land for 100 leagues west of the Cape Verde Islands, and the lands beyond that to Spain. For some reason Portugal protested, and at the risk of war with Spain brought about a revision of that treaty, in 1494, which gave Portugal the lands for 370 leagues west of the Cape Verde Islands.

According to Las Casas, the King of Portugal had definite information which led him to make this demand. Batalha-Reis quotes Las Casas, as writing from Columbus' own diaries and reports, in 1498, before the trip on which he discovered the mainland of South America:

"The admiral says again that he wants to go south, as he believes... he will be able to find islands and lands ... and because he wants to see what was the meaning of King D. João of Portugal when he said that there was *terra firma* to the south; and for this reason he [Columbus] says that the King of Portugal had differences with the kings of Castile, which were settled when it was decided that the King of Portugal should have 370 leagues to the west, beyond the islands of the Azores and Cape Verde." [24]

Las Casas adds that inhabitants of the Cape Verde Islands told Columbus "that canoes had been known to go from the Guinean coast to the west with merchandise." This comment from Columbus' diaries or reports presents an interesting vista of one connection between east and west.

The natives of Haiti are said to have told Columbus that other white men had been there previously.[25]

Leo Wiener in his two-volume work on *Africa and the Discovery of America* throws further light on this point. He states that in his journal of his third voyage Columbus relates:

Before starting for Hispaniola he was told by King Juan of Portugal that ships had come from the coast of Guinea [west Africa] with merchandise to the islands of the west, and so he decided first to go to Guinea "to verify on his way the opinion of King Don Juan, and he wanted to find out what the Indians of Hispaniola had told him, that there had come to it from the south and southeast Negro people, who brought those spear points made of a metal which they called *guanín,* of which he had sent to the King and Queen for assaying. . . ." There is no escaping the fact that Columbus knew that the guaní came from Guinea and that there had been merchants or voyagers in Hispaniola before him. This confirms our derivation of *caona,* guani from the Mande word for "gold." [The Mande or Mandingos are one of the major west African peoples. At that time theirs was a powerful kingdom, its capital being the trading center for a vast area.] [26]

He further states that "the very alloy is of African origin.[27]

Wiener discusses at great length the evidences of pre-Columbian contact between Africa and America. Some of his conclusions are: "The accumulated evidence is overwhelmingly in favor of an introduction of the articles under discussion [tobacco, cotton, shell-money] from Africa, by European and Negro traders, decades earlier than 1492." [28] Also:

We are again brought back to the transference to America of African commerce, of which we have heard so much. The bread roots [manioc, etc.], tobacco, wampum, all proceeded in their dissemination in America along the same roads. The only question is to determine the date of the first contact. There can be little doubt that in some things the African influence was exerted before Columbus, and that this influence could not have existed before the XI. century. . . . Most likely the Mandingos reached America in the middle of the XV. century, with the Portuguese explorers, but should it be possible to prove that the French traders had reached America from the Guinea coast, where they were found already at the end of the XIV. century, the first contact of Africa and America may be set back another half a century.[29]

He concludes: "From Africa the tobacco found its way into America, half a century, possibly a century, before the so-called discovery." [30]

Charles E. Nowell, summing up numerous items of evidence in his "Discovery of Brazil—Accidental or Intentional?" concludes: "To avoid a tedious enumeration of all the pre-Columbian voyages westward from Portugal and the islands, it is enough to say that the list of such achievements is long." He states:

The Catholic Sovereigns, in a letter addressed to Columbus, September 5, 1493, stated that Portuguese diplomats had let slip certain information about such lands to the southwest. Columbus knew that the Portuguese stand at Tordesillas [where the treaty of 1494 for division of territory between Portugal and Spain was made] was based upon some knowledge, as his third voyage demonstrates.[31]

Nowell further proceeds:

In 1498, while Gama's fate was still unknown [Vasco da Gama had sailed for India around Africa in 1496], the King sent Duarte Pacheco Pereira to make a voyage of investigation along the South American coast. In fulfilling his orders, Pacheco anticipated Pedro Alvares Cabral by two years.[32]

Proceeding in secrecy because of Spanish jealousy, [he] once and for all verified the existence and location of South America.[33]

Nowell adds that in 1505 Pacheco wrote a treatise addressed to King Manoel of Portugal, mentioning his discovery of South America in 1498, a mainland, he said, extending 70° north and 28½° south from the equator, and that "at neither extremity has its termination or cape been seen." [34] This account was not published until 1892, and "now finds unquestioned acceptance."

As we come to the time when voyages, if made, might have furnished more immediate information to Thomas More, we find that the evidence of such possibility continues to accumulate.

In May, 1499, Amerigo Vespucci and Hojeda sailed from Spain. During their year's absence they explored the South American coast, mostly north of the equator, and went as far northwest as about the east coast of Florida. On this voyage Juan de la Cosa, one of those in charge of a ship, prepared a map of part of South America. On this map the most conspicuous feature in the interior of the continent is a large lake, which may have been intended to represent Lake Titicaca in the land of the Incas, the largest lake in South America. As other explorers reported in succeeding years,[35] there were rumors of such a fabulous lake, a center of great wealth. The body of water shown on La Cosa's map is larger and farther north than Titicaca, but the location is perhaps as close as could be learned by hearsay through natives who were obliged to communicate their information largely by signs.

The belief in Portugal that there were lands to the west is reflected by concessions given by King John II in 1484, eight years before Columbus' first trip, to Fernão Domingues do Arco of Madeira. He also gave concessions of those lands to Fernão Dulmo of Terceira in 1486, and to Dulmo and João Afonso do Estreito in 1487.[36] These royal concessions for lands across the Atlantic probably had some basis in actual knowledge.

The grant to Fernão Dulmo in 1486 was for "the grant of a great island or islands, or stretch of continental coast, presumed to be the island of the Seven Cities, which he hoped to find." [37] This grant was made after King John of

Portugal refused the exacting terms demanded by Columbus for exploration across the Atlantic.

Destruction of the records of Dieppe in France by fire some centuries ago may have done away with other records of early discovery. There is a tradition in Dieppe that prominent merchants there arranged for one Jean Cousin to go on a voyage of exploration in 1488. From the Azores he was carried to the west by an ocean current and arrived at the mouth of an immense river. From there he sailed to south Africa, discovered Cape Agulhas, the southern tip of Africa, and returned, arriving in 1499. Recently a document was found—evidence in a trial—which tends to confirm this tradition. In 1537 it was attempted to prove that in 1531 ships visited "Fernambuquo, a port of Brazil, where was a castle made by El Rey, our lord, and his Portuguese vassals thirty years ago and more." [38]

Prestage states that "an expedition under Gonçalo Coelho went out [from Portugal] in 1503 which followed the Brazilian coast down to the Rio de Cananea and is referred to by Goes in a single paragraph." [39]

In December, 1499, Vicente Yanez Pinzon, who had commanded one of Columbus' vessels in 1492, sailed with four vessels, and in February, 1500, reached Brazil at about 10° south. From there he explored the coast northward to Costa Rica, and thus returned by way of Haiti (Hispaniola), reaching Spain in September, 1500.

A more interesting voyage for our purposes was that of Pedro Álvares Cabral. In 1500 he sailed from Portugal with thirteen ships, ostensibly for India by going around Africa, though in the opinion of some he purposely sailed for South America,[40] reaching the coast of Brazil two years after Pereira, ten months after Vespucci, five months after Pinzon, and two and a half months after de Lepe, all these others, except Pereira, having sailed from Spain. There are several interesting points to his voyage.

Cabral sailed by instructions given him by Vasco da Gama, who had just returned from his famous first trip around Africa to Asia. These instructions, which called for sailing westward across the Atlantic to near the coast of South America in order to take advantage of favoring winds and currents, and thence southeasterly to the Cape of Good Hope, required thousands of miles of extra travel as compared with a direct route. Samuel Eliot Morison, in his *Portuguese Voyages to America in the Fifteenth Century,* enlarges on the excellence of these instructions, saying they could not be bettered today after four centuries of sailing experience. He states, "How marvellous and worthy of highest praise that the Portuguese, after one Cape voyage (that of Dias) near to the African coast, and another (da Gama's) further out, should have discovered the means of using the brave winds of the South Atlantic to the best advantage!" [41]

Morison is one of those who hold that no Portuguese trips were taken except those for which definite records exist. He states, "That there was no Portuguese voyage to Brazil befor Cabral's [1500] seems certain." [42] But which view taxes our credulity less—to think that a single trip by da Gama into the western Atlantic should result in sailing instructions by a roundabout route that cannot be bettered today, or to assume that such thorough knowledge of ocean currents and winds and seasons as was evidenced by later voyagers was the gradual accumulation of considerable sailing experience in that region?

There is a still more interesting point concerning this voyage of Cabral. On reaching the coast of Brazil in 1500 he sent back two of his thirteen ships to report to the King of Portugal. Two letters to the King from shipmasters were entrusted to these returning vessels. One of them, by a Master John, contains some surprising information. Quoting from Greenlee's translation:

As regards the situation of this land, Señor, Your Highness should order a *mappa mundi* to be brought which Pero Vaaz Bisagudo has, and on it Your Highness will be able to see the location of this land. That *mappa mundi*, however, does not show whether this land is inhabited or not. It is an old *mappa mundi*, and there Your Highness will also find la Mina marked.[43]

An "old" map of Brazil in 1500!

One other item in this letter is interesting. The fleet carried 20 convicts which they left along the route. One of the descriptions sent back to Brazil contained the following passage:

I believe, Senhor, that with these two convicts who remain here, there stay also two seamen who to-night left this ship, fleeing to shore in a skiff. They have not come back and we believe that they remain here, because to-morrow, God willing, we take our departure from here.[44]

It seems that leaving men behind, as described in the so-called Vespucci letter concerning his "fourth" voyage, and by Thomas More in *Utopia*, was not an unheard-of action.

Greenlee further quotes from a manuscript in the Ricordiana Library (MS 1910) a passage which indicates activities which have not been generally known. The manuscript is a letter from Piero Rondinelli, written from Seville in October, 1502. The translation reads:

And the King of Portugal leased the lands which were discovered for him [in Brazil] to certain New Christians [Christianized Jews] and they are obliged each year to send six small ships and to discover each year three hundred leagues farther and to build a fortress in the land discovered and to remain there three years, and the first year they are to pay nothing and the second one-sixth and the third one-fourth, and they agree to carry enough brazil-wood and slaves, and perhaps they will find here other profitable things.[45]

Perhaps the fortress referred to in the Dieppe trial was one they built.

Another early contact with the Brazilian coast was that of da Gama. In Robertson's notes on Magellan's voyage we read: "Vasco da Gama (on his second voyage, 1502-1503) . . . . ere doubling the Cape of Good Hope, crossed to the Brazilian coast, which they followed as far as Cape Santo Agostinho." [46]

Nowell sums up the situation:

Cabral, who was but the central figure in a series of explorations, formed the connecting link between those mariners who had clandestinely preceded him and those who were to bring his country's work to fulfilment in Brazil.[47]

Greenlee states concerning the year of Cabral's Portuguese voyage:

Five Spanish fleets may have sailed during the year 1499, under the commands of Alonzo de Ojeda (who it is said was accompanied by Amerigo Vespucci as a merchant and by Juan de la Cosa as pilot), Cristobal Guerra, Vincente Yañez Pinzon (who had gone with Columbus on his first voyage), and Diego de Lepe. Some believe that there should be added the name of Alonso Vellez de Mendoza.[48]

Even where there are no recorded descriptions, some surviving maps and globes throw strong light on the probability of several trips to South America early enough to allow Thomas More to have received the information presented in his *Utopia.*

The first map to bear the name America is the Waldseemüller map of 1507, a map of the world which accompanied the supposed descriptions of Vespucci's four voyages. Any information on this map concerning the west coast of South America must have been gained at least a year or more before that date, seven years before Balboa discovered the

Pacific at Panama, thirteen years before Magellan sailed around South America, and more than twenty years before Pizarro "discovered" Peru.

So far as surviving records throw light on the matter, the Waldseemüller map gives no supporting evidence as to the west coast of South America. Yet the detail showing a small outline map of upper South America (see end-paper, right-hand map), shows a remarkably good generalized outline of the west coast, decidedly better than on most maps published from twenty-five to seventy-five years later, which commonly showed South America as shaped about like an equilateral triangle. This map suggests strongly that someone from Europe had visited the west coast; or that, since the outline is very much generalized with no pretense of representing an actual shoreline, it might have been drawn from information received along the east coast indirectly by way of Indian traders.

The main map of South America in Waldseemüller's map of the world (see end-paper, left-hand map) also is suggestive. From the lower end of South America it shows an actual coastline north to about 40°, with close approximation to accuracy when we consider the difficulty a navigator would have in distinguishing the true coastline and its tortuous peninsulas from a chain of coastal islands. From about 40° latitude toward the north there is no pretense of showing an actual coast. The implication is that the coast had been actually explored as far north as 40°. Mountains are correctly shown along the coast as far north as the actual coastline is delineated. To assume that all this accurate representation is a matter of sheer chance or imagination is straining credulity.

Vespucci describes his voyage of 1501 for four thousand miles along the east coast of South America to about latitude 50° south, or within less than 300 miles of the Strait of Magellan. That was only about three days' sailing distance. In view of the great secrecy concerning important discoveries which was imposed upon explorers under Portuguese auspices it seems not impossible that Vespucci found out more than is told in the few letters of his which survive. May he not have passed through the Strait of Magellan and for a distance up the west cost of South America, and may it not be that the relatively accurate map of the lower west coast was made from his confidential records? Vespucci wrote that he had sent a full account of his voyage to the King of Portugal. If he did so, this, like most other such records, has been lost.

The "Jagellonicus" Globe of 1510 showed the south terminus of South America at about 56°, the correct latitude for Cape Horn. On the "Lenox" globe, the date of which is variously estimated from 1503 to 1510, the southern terminus of South America also is correctly indicated, and the lower west coast is shown with approximate accuracy. The Glareanus southern hemisphere map (1510-1520) reproduced in Lawrence Wroth's *Early Cartography of the Pacific*, shows the southern terminus of South America at about 50°.

In the same volume, and in letters to the author, Wroth discusses an early German pamphlet, *Copia der Newen Zeytung ausz Presillg Landt*, describing a voyage sent out by Christoval de Haro. Wroth believes it has been conclusively shown that this voyage returned to Lisbon in 1514, and that the expedition reached the La Plata, but did not get to the Strait of Magellan. From Humboldt's French version of the pamphlet [49] the following is translated:

You will also learn with pleasure that the travelers announce that they have obtained, 200 leagues from the Cape, in the direction of Europe (toward the east), at the mouth of a stream, ideas about much silver, gold and copper which is in the interior of the country. They even state that the commander of the other ship will bring to the king of Portugal a silver axe. Ordinary axes are generally made of stone. They also bring a metal of the color of brass which does not take on rust; they do not know what this metal is, perhaps gold of a low alloy. They heard about a people in the mountains, rich in gold armor made of very thin plates of gold. The combatants wear it on the chest and on the forehead. The captain is bringing with him an inhabitant of this country who very much wants to see the king of Portugal, and tell him that he is in a position to procure for him as much gold and silver as the ships can carry. The inhabitants of this coast have told that from time to time they see other vessels arriving whose crews wear clothing like ours and nearly all of whom have red (blond) beards. The Portuguese believe, from these signs, that they are French: they even pretend that they are *Gezyner* (Aigeuner? Bohemiens?) who sail toward Malaqua; for it is known that at Malaqua there is a better trade in silver and in copper than in our country. That is all the most recent news. The ship (which has already arrived) is loaded, below decks, with Brazilian wood; on deck are the youths and girls bought for very little by the Portuguese, for a large number embarked quite willingly.

This pamphlet in "crabbed German style" from the archives of the great German trading firm of the Fuggers is evidence of a voyage along the South American coast which returned in time to supply Thomas More with information, and which brought specific news of the Incas. Wroth adds that the date of this account is indicated by the fact that Schöner used it in preparing his little treatise to accompany his globe of 1515. Wroth comments: "It is not at all unlikely that there was a great deal of information floating around which More could have picked up." It is significant that this account speaks of earlier voyages to this coast "from time to time" by Europeans who, it seems, were not Portuguese.

A. E. Nordenskiöld states of the so-called "Schöner's

globe": "It is evidently founded on a voyage along the eastern coast of South America, which would be perfectly unknown if it had not, as mentioned above, been occasionally referred to in some insignificant geographical pamphlets." He states that the authority of Schöner's globe "was derived from some charts now lost, on which the delineation of the South American continent deviated from all other maps." [50]

There is another bit of strong evidence to the effect that there were voyages of exploration of which few if any records remain. Concerning Magellan's trip, Las Casas, his contemporary, wrote: "Magellan had a well painted globe, which exhibited the entire earth, and he showed thereby the route which he thought of taking, but with intention he had left the strait blank so that no one might learn his secret." [51] Also, Pigafetta, who sailed with Magellan and kept an extensive journal of the voyage, wrote:

Had it not been for the captain-general [Magellan], we would not have found that strait, for we all thought and said that it was closed on all sides. But the captain-general who knew where to sail to find a well-hidden strait, which he saw depicted on a map in the treasury of the king of Portugal, which was made by that excellent man, Martin de Boemia,* sent two ships . . . to discover what was inside the cape de la baia. [52]

A. E. Nordenskiöld in his *Facsimile Atlas* describes two pamphlets printed at least five years before Magellan's trip which yet expressly state "that the New World ends to the South with a cape surrounded by a strait, similar to that of Gibraltar." [53]

---

* The famous Behaim globe, which contains many errors, was made between 1491 and 1493 at Nuremburg. In 1493 Behaim (the name has varied spellings) returned to Lisbon, and from 1494 to 1506 lived in the Azores. Then he returned to Lisbon, where he died on July 29, 1506. There are myths that he visited America before Columbus, and the Strait of Magellan before Magellan. This strait was sometimes called the "strait of Martin Behaim."

We come finally to the part played by Amerigo Vespucci. In 1504 there was published what purported to be a letter from Vespucci to Soderini, in Florence, describing four voyages to the New World. This publication, or more probably its republication by Waldseemüller and his associates in 1507, seems to be referred to by Thomas More in *Utopia*, when he wrote of his hero, Raphael Hythloday, that he "joined Amerigo Vespucci, and was his constant companion in the three last of those four voyages, which are now universally read; but in the end he did not accompany him home, for he prevailed on Amerigo to let him be one of the twenty-four, who in the last voyage were left at the fort." [54]

This account of the "four voyages" of Vespucci has been the occasion for a vast amount of controversy for four centuries. Until recently he was believed to be its author. It now seems quite certain that Vespucci did not make the first voyage imputed to him. Therefore, if he wrote this letter about the four voyages, he was a lying braggart. Sir Clements Markham, the greatest English authority of his day on this period, thought him to be such. He wrote in 1894, "As there is no doubt that Vespucci wrote the famous letters from Lisbon, we may gather some idea of the man from their contents." [55] He heaped vituperation upon Vespucci, calling him fraud, imposter, juggler, an uneducated ignoramus and liar.

In 1926 there was published in Rome a "Critical Study" of Amerigo Vespucci by Alberto Magnaghi, the gist of which was that the "four letters" constituted a forgery, of which Vespucci was innocent. There has been widespread acceptance of Magnaghi's able research, with the result that Vespucci's reputation is higher today than for centuries past. But what about the "four voyages"? The consensus is that the reports of the "second" and "third" are elaborated and modified accounts of authentic expeditions, that the "first" never took place, and that there are neither supporting nor contradicting data as to the "fourth." Frederick J. Pohl, who in his *Amerigo Vespucci* undertakes to bring the issue up to date, writes:

> As for the alleged "fourth" voyage, no definite record was made of Amerigo's whereabouts in 1503-1504 [the time it was reputed to have been made]. He may have been at sea, but there is no evidence to substantiate the assertion that he was.[56]

Though the first of the four voyages itself probably never was taken, the supposed description of such a voyage contained information actually acquired on a subsequent voyage. Also, the material concerning two of the "four" voyages was taken, with some errors and distortions, from accounts of the actual expeditions. The same may be true of the so-called "fourth" voyage, which would be actually the third; or if, as in case of the "first" voyage, it never occurred, authentic incidents from other voyages, including the account of leaving some of the crew behind, may have been used to make a story. Pohl writes of the account of the "four voyages," "It is credible that the printed versions were pirated from the letters to Lorenzo di Pier Francesco with amplifications added to make a best seller."

It is interesting that More describes Hythloday as having gone on only the last three of the four voyages with Vespucci.* Thus he specifically disclaims his informant's having shared in a voyage which we are nearly certain did not take place. It was none of More's business to argue the falsity of the published report about the first voyage, in the account "which was being read everywhere." It would be

---

* Orbis terrarum contemplandi studio Americo Vespucio se adiunxit, atque in tribus posterioribus illarum quatuor navigationum quae passim iam leguntur, perpetuus eius comes fuit, nisi quod in ultima cum eo non rediit."—*The Utopia of Sir Thomas More, . . . in Latin from the edition of March 1518*, etc., by J. H. Lupton, Oxford, Clarendon Press, 1895.

enough for him to indicate that his man Hythloday went on voyages which did actually take place. There was a motive for the author of the four voyages to add the "first" voyage, as it made Vespucci appear to reach the continent before Columbus. There seems no such incentive for forging an account of the fourth voyage, which was the least dramatic of all.

Even today the controversy concerning Vespucci's voyages is not finished. Since the publication of Magnaghi's work another letter, presumably by Vespucci, written in 1502 and describing his so-called third voyage, has been unearthed by Professor Roberto Ridolfi, who holds it to be genuine, while Magnaghi disputes its authenticity.[57] In this case the decision seems to rest with Magnaghi, but when we realize that the discoveries and studies of the past twenty-five years have very greatly changed the opinions of scholars concerning Vespucci, it seems probable that we have not yet reached the last chapter. Other letters may yet appear.

The present state of the issue is that the so-called fourth voyage of Vespucci (actually it would be the third) has been neither proved nor disproved. Whether Thomas More in fact might have received information from a man who went on that particular voyage cannot therefore be asserted or denied with finality.

From the accounts we have referred to relating to early voyages to South America it seems reasonably certain that, even in case Vespucci did not take the so-called fourth voyage, there were various other possibilities by which More might have received information concerning Peru. More did not hesitate to take the liberties of an author, and if it would have furthered his ends to attribute his information to the source then most in the public mind, the "four voyages," he probably would have done so.

If More did get his information from a traveler as he stated, then he evidently had some doubts of its authenticity himself, for he carefully guarded himself against being made a fool of by learned men. In his letter to Giles which served as a sort of introduction to *Utopia*, he wrote:

> I do not pretend that if I had determined to write about the commonwealth and had remembered such a story, I should have shrunk from a fiction, by which the truth, as if smeared with honey, might more pleasantly flow into men's minds. But if I wanted to abuse the ignorance of common folk I should certainly have been careful to prefix some indications for the learned to see through my purpose. Thus if I had put nothing but the names of prince, river, city and island such as might suggest to the learned that the island was nowhere, the city a phantom, the river without water, and the prince without a people, this would not have been hard to do, and would have been much wittier than what I did; for if the faithfulness of an historian had not been binding on me, I am not so stupid as to have preferred to use those barbarous and meaningless names, Utopia, Anyder, Amaurote and Ademus.[58]

For "Utopia" is Greek for "nowhere," "Anyder" for "without water," etc., while "Hythloday" means "learned in nonsense." Yet even here, his remark, "If I had remembered such a story," implies that it was not solely his own creation.

Having suggested the range of these possibilities, since there is no evidence that Vespucci did not take the trip, and since the information included in the supposed "second" and "third" of the "four" voyages proves to be generally accurate, we have proceeded with our account on the assumption that the report is similarly accurate for the so-called fourth voyage. The similarity of *Utopia* to the actualities of Peru constitutes, we believe, strong internal evidence that More had a source of information, probably very much as he described.

NOTES

Chapter I. Model for Utopia

1. William H. Prescott, *The History of the Conquest of Peru*. New York, 1847. The edition used is in *The Complete Works of William Hickling Prescott*, edited by John Foster Kirk in 12 vols. London, Gibbings & Company, 1896. Hereafter cited as *Conquest of Peru*.

2. Clements Robert Markham, *The Incas of Peru*. New York, E. P. Dutton and Company, 1910.

3. Philip Ainsworth Means, *Ancient Civilizations of the Andes*. New York, Charles Scribner's Sons, 1931.

4. Philip Ainsworth Means, "A Re-Examination of Prescott's account of Early Peru," *The New England Quarterly*, IV (October, 1931), 661.

5. *Ancient Civilizations of the Andes*, p. 286.

6. *Ibid.*, pp. 288-89.

7. *Conquest of Peru*, I, 70.

8. *Ibid.*, I, 75

9. *Ancient Civilizations of the Andes*, p. 350.

10. *Conquest of Peru*, I, 57-58, 159.

Chapter II. On the Trail of Utopian Sources

1. Erland Nordenskiöld, "The Guarani Invasion of the Inca Empire in the Sixteenth Century," *Geographical Review*, I (July-December, 1917), 103-21.

2. *Conquest of Peru*, I, 46, 47-48, 51.

3. *Ibid.*, p. 46. Means, however, makes the comment that the Inca Empire was "Theoretically a state wherein no private property existed but practically one in which there was in fact quite a considerable private property in a moral, if not in a legal, sense."—*Ancient Civilizations of the Andes*, p. 302.

4. Thomas More, *Utopia*. Translation by Gilbert Burnet, 1684. Reprinted, with capitalization, spelling, and punctuation modernized, in *Ideal Empires and Republics*, edited by Charles M. Andrews. New York and London, M. Walter Dunne, Publisher, 1901. Unless otherwise noted, all quotations are from this edition. Hereafter cited as *Utopia*.

5. *Equality* (New York, 1897; edition used, New York, D. Appleton-Century Company, 1934), p. 27.

6. *Conquest of Peru*, I, 53.

7. *Ancient Civilizations of the Andes*, pp. 300, 301.

8. *Utopia*, pp. 163-64.

9. *Equality*, p. 302.

10. *Conquest of Peru*, I, 52, 55-56, 50, 51, 52.

11. *Ancient Civilizations of the Andes*, pp. 325-26.

12. *Utopia*, p. 179.

13. *Conquest of Peru*, I, 50, 54-55.

14. *Utopia*, p. 174.

15. Edward Bellamy, *Looking Backward 2000-1887* (Boston, 1888; edition used, Boston, Houghton Mifflin Company, 1926), p. 106.

16. *Ancient Civilizations of the Andes*, p. 325.

17. *Ibid.*, p. 251.

18. *Conquest of Peru*, I, 157.

19. *Utopia*, pp. 164, 166, 175, 228.

20. *Looking Backward*, p. 87.

21. *Ancient Civilizations of the Andes*, p. 294.

22. *Utopia*, p. 171.

23. *Looking Backward*, p. 63.

24. *Conquest of Peru*, I, 53, 156.

25. *Utopia*, p. 169.
26. *Looking Backward*, pp. 67-68.
27. *Conquest of Peru*, I, 53, 54.
28. *Utopia*, pp. 169, 173.
29. *Ancient Civilizations of the Andes*, pp. 298-99.
30. *Utopia*, p. 221.
31. *Looking Backward*, pp. 156, 157.
32. *Conquest of Peru*, I, 150, 50.
33. *Utopia*, p. 169.
34. *Conquest of Peru*, I, 53.
35. *Utopia*, p. 169.
36. *Conquest of Peru*, I, 58.
37. Philip Ainsworth Means, *Fall of the Inca Empire and the Spanish Rule in Peru: 1530-1780* (New York, Charles Scribner's Sons, 1932), p. 11.
38. *Utopia*, pp. 228, 175, 230.
39. *Looking Backward*, p. 90.
40. *Ibid.*, p. 201.
41. *Conquest of Peru*, I, 4, 123-24, 125-26, 129.
42. *Utopia*, pp. 195, 166.
43. *Conquest of Peru*, I, 51, 122-23.
44. *Utopia*, p. 168.
45. *Ancient Civilizations of the Andes*, pp. 344-45.
46. *Utopia*, p. 174.
47. *Conquest of Peru*, I, 43, 45.
48. *Looking Backward*, pp. 202, 208.

CHAPTER III. NON-UTOPIAN PARALLELS

1. *Conquest of Peru*, I, 157.
2. *Utopia*, pp. 178-79.
3. R. W. Chambers, *Thomas More* (New York, Harcourt, Brace and Company, 1935), p. 137.
4. *Ibid.*, p. 396.
5. R. W. Chambers, *The Saga and the Myth of Sir Thomas*

More, from the *Proceedings* of the British Academy (London, Oxford University Press, 1927), p. 29.

6. William Edward Campbell, *More's Utopia and His Social Teaching* (London, Eyre and Spottiswoode Limited, 1930), pp. 117, 118.

7. *Looking Backward,* p. 71.

8. Lewis Mumford, *The Story of Utopias* (New York, Boni and Liveright, 1922), pp. 72, 72-73.

9. *Conquest of Peru,* I, 150, 70, 66-67.

10. *Ancient Civilizations of the Andes,* p. 303.

11. *Utopia,* pp. 208, 209, 210.

12. *Conquest of Peru,* I, 150-51.

13. *Utopia,* p. 184.

14. *Conquest of Peru,* I, 74-75, 117.

15. *Ibid.,* I, 145.

16. *Ancient Civilizations of the Andes,* p. 319.

17. *Utopia,* pp. 165, 166.

18. *Conquest of Peru,* I, 30, 31-32.

19. *Utopia,* p. 220.

20. *Conquest of Peru,* I, 90-91.

21. *Utopia,* p. 224.

22. *Conquest of Peru,* I, 121.

23. *Utopia,* p. 220.

24. J. H. Lupton, *The Utopia of Sir Thomas More, with additional translations, introductions, and notes, in Latin from the edition of March 1518, and from the first English translation of 1551* (Oxford, Clarendon Press, 1895), pp. 3, 5-9.

25. *More's Utopia and His Social Teaching,* pp. 95, 96.

26. *Ancient Civilizations of the Andes,* p. 309.

27. *The Incas of Peru,* pp. 166, 168-69.

28. William Vogt, "Hunger at the Peace Table," *Saturday Evening Post,* May 12, 1945.

CHAPTER IV. HYTHLODAY, FIRST CIRCUMNAVIGATOR?

1. Ralph Linton, *Archeology of the Marquesas Islands*, Honolulu, Bishop Museum, Bulletin 23, 1925.

2. Roland B. Dixon, "The Problem of the Sweet Potato in Polynesia," *American Anthropologist*, N.S. Vol. XXXIV, No. 1 (January-March, 1932). See also Roland B. Dixon, "The Long Voyages of the Polynesians," *Proceedings of the American Philosophical Society* (Philadelphia), Vol. LXXIV, No. 1 (July, 1934).

3. *The Travels of Sir John Mandeville* (written in French and published between 1357 and 1371. Edition cited here, London, Macmillan and Company, 1923), pp. 123-24.

4. *Ibid.*, pp. 122-23.

5. Emile Montegut, "Sir John Mandeville," *Revue des Deux Mondes.* Translated by Mrs. R. W. Latimer, in *Littell's Living Age*, CLXXXIV (March 22, 1890), 741. (M. Montegut quotes Mr. Thomas Wright.)

CHAPTER V. THE ORIGINS OF UTOPIA

1. Aristophanes, *The Ecclesiazusae.* English translation of Benjamin B. Rogers (London, William Heinemann; New York, G. P. Putnam's Sons, 1924), pp. 299-303, 309-15. Reprinted by permission of the publisher.

2. Amos 7: 14, 15.

3. *Ibid.*, 8: 4, 5, 6, 8, 10.

4. *Ibid.*, 9: 2.

5. *Ibid.*, 5: 14, 24.

6. *Ibid.*, 9: 13, 14, 15.

7. Isaiah 2: 4.

8. *Ibid.*, 65: 21, 22, 25.

9. From a letter to the author.

10. Waterman, *Royal Correspondence of the Assyrian Empire*, Part I, Letter 2.

11. From a letter to the author.

12. From a letter to the author.

13. *Dialogues of the Buddha,* translated by T. W. Rhys Davids and Wife (London, Oxford University Press, 1921), Pt. III, p. 73.

14. *The Sacred Books of the East* edited by Max Müller (Oxford, Clarendon Press, 1885), XXVII, 364-66.

15. *Ibid.,* pp. 210-48.

16. From a letter to the author.

17. This has been translated by Chi-Chen Wang, of Columbia University. Aside from a few of the chapters, from which the succeeding information was received, it has not been published in English.

18. *The Poetic Edda,* translated from the Icelandic with an Introduction and Notes by Henry Adams Bellows (New York, the American Scandinavian Foundation, 1923), st. 23, p. 11. Reprinted by permission of the publisher.

19. *Ibid.,* st. 45, pp. 19-20.

20. *Ibid.,* st. 57, p. 24.

21. *Ibid.,* st. 59, p. 24.

22. *Ibid.,* st. 61, p. 25.

23. *Ibid.,* st. 62, p. 25.

24. *Ibid.,* st. 64, p. 26.

25. From a letter to the author.

26. J. O. Hertzler, *A History of Utopian Thought,* New York, The Macmillan Company, 1926.

27. *The Travels of Sir John Mandeville,* pp. 192-93.

28. *Ibid.,* p. 194.

29. Quoted in Arthur O. Lovejoy and George Boas, *Primitivism and Related Ideas in Antiquity* (Baltimore, The Johns Hopkins Press, 1935), pp. 338-39. Hereafter cited as Lovejoy and Boas, *Primitivism.* Reprinted by permission of the publisher.

30. Frederic Seebohm, *The Oxford Reformers* (New York, E. P. Dutton and Company, Inc., 1914 [Everyman Edition]), p. 216.

31. *Proceedings and Transactions of the Royal Society of Canada*, XXX (1936), 57-59.

CHAPTER VI. THE GOLDEN AGE

1. Quoted in Lovejoy and Boas, *Primitivism*, p. 27.
2. Quoted *ibid*, pp. 40-41.
3. *Encyclopedia of Religion and Ethics* (New York, Charles Scribner's Sons, 1928), I, 195.
4. *Ibid.*, pp. 194-95.
5. Quoted in Lovejoy and Boas, *Primitivism*, p. 67.
6. Quoted *ibid.*, pp. 310-11.
7. *Ibid.*, pp. 326-27.
8. Charles M. Doughty, *Travels in Arabia Deserta* (New York, Boni and Liveright, n.d.), I, 345, 318, 248-49.
9. Lovejoy and Boas, *Primitivism*, p. 289.
10. Such studies as that of the Winnebagos in *Primitive Man as Philosopher*, by Paul Radin (New York, D. Appleton and Company, 1927), and of the Hopi Indians, in *The Hopi Way*, by Laura Thompson and Alice Joseph (University of Chicago Press, 1944), are examples.
11. Dudley Tyng, "The Confucian Utopia," *Journal of the American Oriental Society*, LIV (1934), 67-69. Quoted from James Legge's translation of *Li Ki*, in *The Sacred Books of the East*, XXVII, 364-67.
12. Clifton Fadiman, ed., *I Believe* (Simon and Schuster, 1939), pp. 255, 256, 257-58, 266, 267, 267-68, 269, 270, 271, 275-76. Similar descriptions are given in *The Eskimos: Their Environment and Folkways*, by Edward Moffat Weyer, Jr. (New Haven, Yale University Press, 1932); *Tales and Traditions of the Eskimo*, by Dr. Henry Rink (Edinburgh and London, Wm. Blackwood and Sons, 1875); and *Greenland by the Polar Sea*, by Knud Rasmussen (London, William Heinemann, 1921), translated from the Danish by Asta and Rowland Kenney. Quotations from *I Believe* reprinted by permission.

13. P. Kolben, *The Present State of the Cape of Good Hope*, Done into English by Mr. Medley (London, W. Innys, 1631), pp. 165, 262.

14. Margaret Mead, ed., *Coöperation and Competition among Primitive Peoples* (New York, McGraw-Hill Book Company, 1937), pp. 28, 29, 31, 40, 41-42, 46, 49-50. Reprinted by permission.

15. Oliver J. Thatcher, ed., *The Ideas That Have Influenced Civilization* (Milwaukee, Roberts-Manchester Publishing Company, 1901), V, 377.

16. Edward Bellamy, *The Blindman's World and Other Stories* (Boston, Houghton Mifflin and Company, 1898), pp. 398-99, 403-5, 410, 412.

17. Quoted from H. A. Giles, *Gems of Chinese Literature*, (Shanghai, Kelly and Walsh, 1922), pp. 250-53, and from "Flowers in the Mirror," an unpublished translation by Chi-Chen Wang of the *Ching Hua Yüan*.

18. Baltasar Gracian, *A Truthtelling Manual and the Art of Worldly Wisdom*, translated by Martin Fischer (Springfield, Ill., Charles C. Thomas, 1934), p. 139.

19. *Ibid.*, p. 173.

20. *Equality*, p. 265.

Chapter VIII. Why Utopias Fail

1. Quoted in John Minter Morgan, *The Revolt of the Bees* (London, Longman, Rees, Orme, Brown, and Green, 1826), footnotes on pp. 107-8, 143.

2. *Ibid.*, p. 109 n.

3. Samuel Bower, *The Peopling of Utopia* (London, C. Wilkinson, Westgate-Cleave, 1838), p. 4.

4. Don Marquis, *The Almost Perfect State* (Garden City, New York, Doubleday, Page and Company, 1927), pp. 218, 219, 220. Reprinted by permission.

CHAPTER IX. BEYOND UTOPIA

1. Oscar Wilde, *The Soul of Man under Socialism* (Boston, John W. Luce and Company, n.d.), pp. 33-34.

2. Unpublished papers of Edward Bellamy.

3. Ecclesiastes 1: 16, 17.

4. *Ibid.*, 2: 1, 4, 5, 10, 11, 17.

5. Sophocles, *Oedipus, King of Thebes*, translated by Gilbert Murray (New York, Oxford University Press, 1911), p. 71.

6. Edward Bellamy, "Under the Sign Aquarius, editorial in the *Springfield Daily Union*, January 6, 1875.

7. Unpublished papers of Edward Bellamy.

APPENDIX

1. A. E. Nordenskiöld, *Facsimile Atlas to the Early History of Cartography*, translated from the Swedish original (Stockholm, 1889), p. 62.

2. *Ibid.*, pp. 62-63.

3. Charles E. Nowell, "The Discovery of Brazil—Accidental or Intentional?" *Hispanic American Historical Review*, XVI (1936), 337. Hereafter cited as "Discovery of Brazil."

4. Percy Alvin Martin, "Portugal in America," *Hispanic American Historical Review*, XVII (1937), 186.

5. J. Batalha-Reis, "The Supposed Discovery of South America before 1448, and the Critical Methods of the Historians of Geographical Discovery," *The Geographical Journal*, IX (1897), 197. Hereafter cited as "Supposed Discovery of South America."

6. *Ibid.*, p. 199.

7. *The Voyage of Pedro Alvares Cabral to Brazil and India*, from Contemporary Documents and Narratives, translated with Introduction and Notes by William Brooks Greenlee (London, The Hakluyt Society, 2nd series LXXXI (1938), liv.

8. João de Barros, an able and conscientious historian of Portugal, began his history about 1540. He died in 1570. Part of his work was published after his death.

9. Edgar Prestage, "The Search for the Sea Route to India, A.D. 1415-1460," in *Travel and Travellers of the Middle Ages,* edited by Arthur Percival Newton (London, Kegan Paul, Trench, Trubner and Company, Ltd.; New York, Alfred A. Knopf, 1926), pp. 212, 213, 214. Reprinted by permission.

10. *Ibid.,* p. 213.

11. *Ibid.,* p. 198. As illustration of the cosmopolitan character of ships' crews of that day, Magellan's ship-list of 265 men contained the names, and notations of nationality, of Portuguese, Spaniards, Genoese, Italians, Frenchmen, Flemings, Germans, Sicilians, Englishmen, Corfiotes, Malays, Negroes, Moors, Madeirans, and natives of the Azores and Canary Islands.— Antonio Pigafetta, *Magellan's Voyage Around the World,* translated by James Alexander Robertson (Cleveland, Arthur H. Clark Company, 1906), I, 204-16.

12. "Supposed Discovery of South America," p. 210.

13. *The Voyage of Pedro Alvares Cabral,* p. 12 n.

14. See article on "Argentina" in *Encyclopaedia Britannica,* Fourteenth Edition.

15. Erland Nordenskiöld, "Deductions Suggested by the Geographical Distribution of Some Post-Columbian Words Used by the Indians of South America," *Comparative Ethnographic Studies* (Göteborg), V (1922), 9-10, 13.

16. Erland Nordenskiöld, *An Ethno-Geographical Analysis of the Material Culture of Two Indian Tribes of the Gran Chaco* (Gothenburg, 1919), pp. 247-48.

17. *Comparative Ethnographic Studies,* V, 19.

18. *Ibid.,* pp. 24, 25.

19. Philip Ainsworth Means, *The Spanish Main—Focus of Envy, 1492-1700* (New York, Charles Scribner's Sons, 1935), p. 39.

20. "Supposed Discovery of South America," p. 200.

21. *Ibid.*, p. 201.

22. *Ibid.*, p. 203.

23. "Portugal in America," *Hispanic American Historical Review*, XVII (1937), 185. Reprinted by permission.

24. "Supposed Discovery of South America," p. 205.

25. Edgar Prestage, *The Portuguese Pioneers* (London, A. & C. Black, Ltd., 1933), p. 234.

26. Leo Wiener, *Africa and the Discovery of America* (Philadelphia, Innes and Sons, 1920), I, 34. Reprinted by permission.

27. *Ibid.*, II, 117.

28. *Ibid.*, II, Foreword.

29. *Ibid.*, II, 263.

30. *Ibid.*, II, 180. Other authorities are certain that tobacco is a native American plant. A. L. Kroeber in his *Anthropology* gives reasons for that belief. Similar reasons, such as the existence of ancient smoking pipes and the indigenous growth of tobacco, might be adduced, also, to support the theory of African origin.

31. "Discovery of Brazil," pp. 323, 324. Reprinted by permission.

32. *Ibid.*, pp. 324-25.

33. *Ibid.*, p. 338.

34. *Ibid.*, p. 326.

35. See *Voyages and Discoveries in South America*, Done into English from the Originals, being the only Accounts of those Parts hitherto extant (London, printed for S. Buckley, 1698). Part 3 is entitled "The Third [Voyage] from *Cayenne* into *Guinea*, in search of the Lake of Parima, reputed the richest place in the World," by M. Grillet and Bechamel. (Copy in the New York Public Library.)

36. *The Voyage of Pedro Alvares Cabral*, p. lv.

37. Edgar Prestage, *The Portuguese Pioneers*, p. 230.

38. *The Voyage of Pedro Alvares Cabral*, p. lxvi.

39. *The Portuguese Pioneers*, p. 290.

40. See Nowell, "The Discovery of Brazil."

41. Samuel Eliot Morison, *Portuguese Voyages to America in*

the Fifteenth Century (Cambridge, Mass., Harvard University Press, 1940), p. 105.

42. *Ibid.*, p. 141.

43. *The Voyage of Pedro Alvares Cabral*, pp. 37-38. Reprinted by permission.

44. *Ibid*, p. 32.

45. *Ibid.*, p. lxvii n.

46. Pigafetta, *Magellan's Voyage Around the World*, I, 239.

47. "Discovery of Brazil," p. 337.

48. *The Voyage of Pedro Alvares Cabral*, p. lxi.

49. *Examen critique de l'histoire de la Geographie du Nouveau Continent*, (Paris, 1839), V, 243-45.

50. *Facsimile Atlas*, p. 80.

51. Quoted in Edward Luther Stevenson, *Terrestrial and Celestial Globes* . . . (New Haven, Yale University Press, 1921), I, 81.

52. *Magellan's Voyage Around the World*, I, 65.

53. *Facsimile Atlas*, p. 76.

54. Translation by O. C. Richards, Oxford, Basil Blackwood, 1923. These reputed voyages were between 1497 and 1504. The account was printed in 1507. The fort was presumably at Cape Frio in Brazil.

55. Clements R. Markham, trans., *The Letters of Amerigo Vespucci* (London, The Hakluyt Society, 1894), Introduction, p. vii.

56. Frederick J. Pohl, *Amerigo Vespucci: Pilot Major* (New York, Columbia University Press, 1944), p. 154.

57. Letter by Charles E. Nowell in *The Hispanic American Historical Review*, XVIII (1938), 109.

58. Translation by O. C. Richards.

INDEX

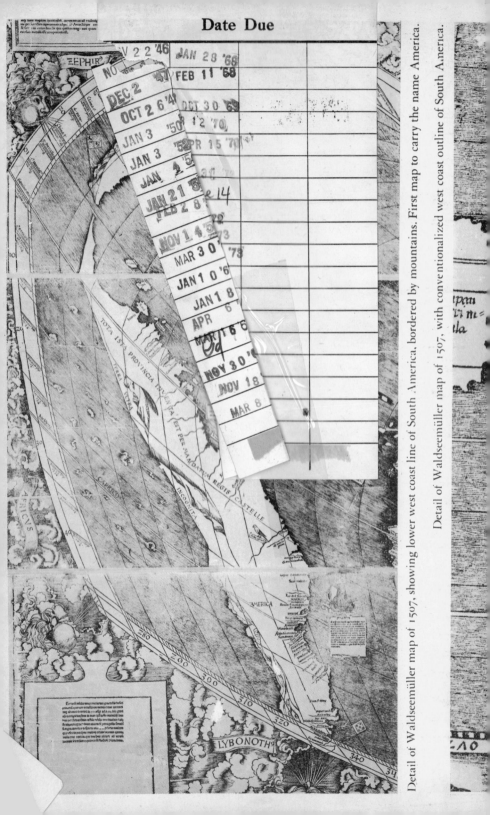

Detail of Waldseemüller map of 1507, showing lower west coast line of South America, bordered by mountains. First map to carry the name America.

Detail of Waldseemüller map of 1507, with conventionalized west coast outline of South America.